CAROLYN J. MULLINS, formerly acting director of the Indiana Center for the Study of Labor in Industrial Society at Indiana University at Bloomington, is now a private communications consultant and teacher of workshops on professional communication. She is the author of Prentice-Hall's highly successful *The Complete Writing Guide to Preparing Reports, Proposals, Memos, Etc.* and *The Complete Manuscript Preparation Style Guide.*

THOMAS W. WEST is director of the Division of Information Systems for The California State University.

Prentice-Hall International, Inc., *London*
Prentice-Hall of Australia Pty. Limited, *Sydney*
Prentice-Hall of Canada Inc., *Toronto*
Prentice-Hall of India Private Limited, *New Delhi*
Prentice-Hall of Japan, Inc., *Tokyo*
Prentice-Hall of Southeast Asia Pte. Ltd., *Singapore*
Whitehall Books Limited, *Wellington, New Zealand*
Editora Prentice-Hall do Brasil LTDA., *Rio de Janerio*

THE OFFICE AUTOMATION PRIMER

Harnessing Information Technologies
For Greater Productivity

CAROLYN J. MULLINS
THOMAS W. WEST

PRENTICE-HALL, INC., Englewood Cliffs, New Jersey 07632

Library of Congress Cataloging in Publication Data

Mullins, Carolyn J.
   The office automation primer.

   "A Spectrum Book."
   Bibliography: p.
   Includes index.
   1. Office practice—Automation.
2. Electronic data processing.   I. West,
Thomas W., date   II. Title.
HF5548.2.M796   1982   651.8'4   82-12986
ISBN 0-13-631085-0
ISBN 0-13-631077-X (pbk.)

This book is available at a special discount when ordered in large quantities. Contact Prentice-Hall, Inc., General Publishing Division, Special Sales, Englewood Cliffs, N. J. 07632.

A SPECTRUM BOOK

ISBN 0-13-631085-0

ISBN 0-13-631077-X (PBK.)

10 9 8 7 6 5 4 3 2 1

Printed in the United States of America

Editorial/production/design supervision by Shirley Covington
Cover design by Jeannette Jacobs
Manufacturing buyer: Barbara Frick

For those who count most in our lives—our families:

Nick, Nick, Rob, and Nancy
Lynn, Susan, Cynthia, Steven, and Sara

Contents

1 People + Hardware + Software = Modern Office Systems

IS THIS IN YOUR FUTURE?

Managers *start the day by signing onto desktop terminals to check their calendars and act on documents in their electronic "in-baskets." They send memos, correct and print drafts of reports, set up meetings, and pore over management reports—all without touching a pencil or paper or leaving their desks.*

Personnel officers *start by checking appointments, checking and sending memos, correcting and printing reports, listing the day's tasks for secretaries, and asking for records on the day's interviewees.*

Administrative support staff *sign on to their work stations and review the day's work. One requests mailing labels for a promotional letter. Another prepares the form letter of request, which will "merge" with the mailing list to address each letter personally. A third confirms meetings and writes several memos and letters—again, without touching pencil or paper or leaving the station.*

Staff researchers *check and answer mail, send memos to supervisors, write letters, and send reports to one another for review. They*

1

analyze data and incorporate the resulting tables and graphs directly into reports. On a typical morning a researcher might set up an experiment to run and feed data directly into the computer. While it runs, he or she drafts a few pages of one report and makes minor corrections on another—moving one paragraph, deleting another, adding items to the list of references, running the document through the spelling checker, and reviewing the final product before printing.

Students *from elementary school through college do assignments, take tests, evaluate classes, write and print papers, leave notes for teachers, and check library indexes for articles and books on topics they are studying.*

These processes sound like science fiction—yet information technologies that combine word and data processing with telecommunications already make such actions possible. Word processing (WP) and text management by themselves streamline the preparation, filing, retrieving, printing, distributing, and controlling of documents through the interaction of people and machines. For instance, typewriting is easier than printing a letter by hand. Correcting typewriters speed up typing, and proportional spacing enhances the appearance of a printed document. Word processing has evolved from typewriters to MC/STs (Magnetic Card/Selectric Typewriters) and now to electronic logic and computer-assisted devices.

Today, as the vignettes show, the most sophisticated systems are far more than souped-up typewriters. Word processing makes electronic storage and easy retrieval feasible without paper-crammed filing cabinets. When combined with electronic mail and message switching, word processing makes possible instant written communication without the delay of mail service or the need for long-distance telephone calls. A Datapro report (1978, p. 102) summarized these functions with the acronym IPSOD—input, process, storage, output, distribution.

Some systems enable users to do both word and data processing from the same work station. They also enable users to access computerized data bases, graphics packages, photocomposition interfaces, and the like. In fact, the rapid changes in office technologies recently prompted the International Word Processing Association (IWP) to change its name to the International Information/Word Processing Association (the abbreviation remained IWP).

As we noted in the Preface, office productivity is not what it should be, and declining productivity generally has become a national concern. Already, office automation is being touted as a cure for declining office productivity. There are reasons to treat such expectations cautiously. Nevertheless, as our society approaches the twenty-first century, word processing and associated technologies will become increasingly integrated into our way of life. We believe that to maintain management effectiveness and increase organizational efficiency, organizations must plan to integrate all office automation technologies.

TECHNICAL CONSIDERATIONS

The prospects, although promising for increasing office productivity and controlling costs, are not without problems. The root problems are the great variety of products and the lack of standardization. Nearly every vendor's offering has one or more unique features that, you'll be told, are "absolutely essential." Furthermore, no two vendors offer the same complete list of features. The result, predictably, is confusion and heated discussion when managers and staffs try to decide what kind of equipment and software to get.

Joan Thompson, Senior Technical Writer for Jones Manufacturing, fidgeted as she listened. The topic was modern office technology in general and word processing in particular, and the plans being discussed seemed either shortsighted or irrelevant to her professional needs. Across the table, researcher Bill Engle, one of the company's best chemists, seemed equally disturbed.

The group had been discussing the need for features such as word wrap, global search and replace, simultaneous input and printing, automatic decimal centering, spelling dictionaries, automatic page numbering, math packs (which automatically calculate and total columns of figures, thus preventing errors in either hand calculation or transcription), automatic headers and footers, easy reformatting, and so forth. Mary East from the Personal Office wanted "merge" functions for joining letter text with names and addresses in mailing lists.

These features sounded fine, but Thompson wanted more. She often worked on long documents and didn't want to have to worry about running out of file space. Because she often worked with Greek and mathematical symbols, she needed superscripts and subscripts (preferably shown on the screen) and dual-head printers, which accommodate two different printing elements simultaneously. Because she did more revising than drafting, she also wanted automatic marking of texts that have been altered by the most recent revision. Finally, she needed access to data on the main computers, and sometimes she wanted to include computerized data and graphs in documents without retyping. Friends who wrote documentation needed automatic paragraph and outline num-

bering, and automatic tables of contents, lists of tables and illustrations, and indexes.

When the group took a break, she sought out Bill, who turned out to want even more features than she did. "I want electronic mail and a desktop terminal to check and answer mail. I want easy communication with Walter Jones, who works in the West Coast office. I want to be able to write notes to my staff and make work assignments," he said. "I also want to be able to use the same terminal for computer work. Sometimes I want to see an old report. I don't want to send a request and wait weeks. I'd like to be able to tell the computer operator to hang the storage tape for me right away. Most of all, I'd like my own word processing terminal. I'm a lousy typist, but I think best at a keyboard. I like to work a bit, changing as new and better ideas come to me. I use lots of correction fluid just trying to keep drafts clean enough to read. With my own terminal, I could get reports done much faster, and I wouldn't have to keep having drafts retyped. Not to mention having to proofread them over and over again. I get so I can't even find errors, I've seen the words so many times."

"If you think you need a terminal, try being in the PR department," said Thelma Davis. "I'd like word processing with graphics, to draw my illustrations for me, and a photocomposition interface so I could move my text directly into print. Without any errors from rekeyboarding. Our booklets and reports go to everyone from stockholders to customers. We really hear about it when someone finds an error in our work. I'd breathe a lot easier every January if I could get productivity and profits data directly from the computer in table and graph form. Then I'd know the data in the annual report were absolutely correct. Or, if not, that errors were the computer's fault, not mine!"

"Don't leave salespeople out," said Sam Jones, who had flown in from Houston for the meeting. "I'd like to be able to dial in from the field to check supplies, get data on clients, write reports . . ."

These people are among the more sophisticated. They know that somewhere there is equipment that will meet their needs. Many others don't realize that electronic mail can take the drudgery out of scheduling large meetings, that voice-activated computers for Sam already exist, and that teleconferencing is already cutting down on traveling.

High-quality technical solutions exist, but they differ from one firm to the next. Finding the right solution for your firm doesn't require planners that have highly technical training. What is essential, though, is a clear grasp of important concepts, policy directions, study techniques, and short-range planning options. You need to know what questions to ask and how to find answers.

SOCIAL CONSIDERATIONS

Modern office technologies promise to deliver great benefits—but they won't work unless people accept them, and the prospects threaten many persons who don't understand the technology ("techno-resistance," Bentley, 1981) and don't want to lose their jobs. Many also fear changes in office personnel structures.

Therefore, planners must be sensitive to the social dynamics of their firms. No technical solution will work if it is not developed and implemented with the cooperation of staff members. Back in the offices, we can eavesdrop on conversations with a different tone.

"Mark my words," said Florence Smith, who had been the vice president's secretary for 20 years, "it'll never work. Look at all the time they're wasting in that meeting. Then they'll come here with their questionnaires and waste our time trying to find out about 'productivity.' Mr. Longman won't want it, anyway. He dictates to me because he trusts me. He'd never trust a machine, not knowin' who'd be on the other end. Besides, I don't want to learn how to use a computer. This electric typewriter is the only thing I need."

"I hope you're right," said Sue Adams, who had been with the firm six months. "A friend of mine says her office just got word processing and they're now doing the same amount of work with half the staff. We just bought a house, and I don't want to lose my job."

Staff Participation

No matter how good the system or careful the plans, the Smiths, Adamses, and Longmans will sabotage them unless they are brought into the planning, shown the benefits, and assured that the changes won't cost them their jobs. Some executives view technology as "rigid, structured, unforgiving, and unresponsive," and even many data processing personnel have developed a "fortress mentality" resistance to office technology (Scannel, 1980a).

Problems can often be prevented by heading them off. Throughout this book are suggestions for keeping staff members involved in and informed of management thinking and policies as they develop.

Management Support

Office systems specialist R.J. Goldfield (1980a, p. 135) says that top management support is "the single most important criterion for a successful conversion" to office automation. Goldfield cites many cases in which success can be traced directly to firm, explicit support from the top of an organization.

Top management support is important for two reasons. First, as Goldfield notes, it helps to ensure cooperation from staff throughout the organization. Second, as Chapter 2 of this book shows, many of the gains possible with modern office systems are possible only when managers use the systems themselves. The message for managers is: If the support isn't there, plan carefully to develop it. Don't neglect this crucial element in a rush to begin technical studies.

Changes in Staff Size, Structure, and Function

Staff size. Most organizations don't need to fire people as a result of acquiring modern office systems. Staffing changes can be tied to natural turnover. For instance, one of our small office units, knowing in advance that it would be overstaffed, tied its acquisition of a word processor to the resignation of one secretary. One of our large office units acquired its large shared system when it moved to a new building, which made reorganization of the staff much easier.

Sue Adams would stop worrying if someone told her that the only reductions in force will occur naturally, through attrition. She might even become enthusiastic if someone told her that the new technology would open to her many new career possibilities. No longer would her promotions be tied to those of her boss. She could have a career as a WP operator or supervisor, or she could become an administrative support secretary to several managers. She could choose her career path according to her talents.

Smith and her boss will be harder to convince, although that sometimes happens. Very few managers welcome the loss of a private secretary, especially after 20 years. A dictating machine can seem impersonal, and the same administrative support services might not feel the same if rendered by someone who was equally responsible to several managers. When staff members like these are near retirement, the organization's needs can give a bit to accommodate them if they cannot be convinced to cooperate willingly. When the resisters are younger—sometimes the case with managers and staff who lack self-confidence—both sides may have to give a bit. The larger the organization, the greater the flexibility. The greater the support from the top of the organization, the more likely that cooperation will be forthcoming.

Staff structure and function. Modern office systems usually involve restructuring of duties. Often, the traditional secretarial job disappears. The typing becomes the special job of a word processing operator or a correspondence secretary. The administrative parts of the job become the responsibility of an administrative support secretary, who serves two or more managers. When a word processing center is established to centralize typing, a word processing supervisor manages it. Often, though, such centers aren't needed. For instance, in one of our small office units, the heaviest typing responsibilities were given to a person who preferred typing to other secretarial duties, which in turn were moved to another staff member who continued to work in the same office.

The specifics matter less than this: Modern office systems involve people as well as technologies. Managers and staff who ignore the office social system while planning the technical system probably won't succeed.

Quality versus Quantity

Modern technologies enable workers to turn out more in less time. Typists using word processors, especially those whose work involves more time with revisions than with new drafts, experience dramatic increases in productivity. Quality, too, can rise dramatically. In fact, for some organizations, greater quality—value added to current services (Marcus, 1980)—may be more important than productivity gains.

However, the personnel restructuring that often accompanies automation can separate office staff members from one another, often making the word processing operators feel like assembly-line workers. Also, the urge to achieve greater quality can unnecessarily reduce productivity. Managers need to be aware, then, of potential pitfalls and ways to avoid them.

BACKGROUND

Our Purposes

Modern office technology requires management of technology, resources, and people. Our purpose is to provide a framework that will apply no matter what year it is, where your organization is located, or how large it is. We'll tell you what questions to ask and how to get comparable data on word processing systems. We'll give you concepts, methods, and techniques for evaluating modern office technology, especially word processing. The tools aren't complicated, and we don't give detailed technical data. Throughout the book we return to the themes just mentioned: staff participation, changes in the social structure as well as the technology, and the tension between quality and quantity. They are not topics to be treated by themselves but themes that appear and reappear.

The book is for managers, planners, and staff in organizations of all sizes, from the largest to the smallest one-office operation. The concepts, study design, tools, and techniques will work even for offices in which data and word processing take place on the same computer—even it it is a small personal computer.

We use examples liberally. Most refer to the state of information technologies in the spring of 1981, and most are important only as examples of features, processes, or performance, and not as hard-and-fast indicators of quality in a vendor's product. We don't identify many vendors by name. Indeed, if we tried to tell "everything you always wanted to know about" every vendor, the book would be out of date before it was printed because the technology is changing so rapidly.

Our Assumptions

Our basic assumption is that every organization eventually will acquire modern office devices. The important questions, then, are the following:

- When?
- Over what period of time to plan?
- How effectively will the acquisitions meet your organization's short- and long-range needs?

The reasons for this basic assumption are as follows. Individual effectiveness and organizational efficiency (measures of productivity) have always been unstated goals and motivations for using information processing technologies. Since the 1970s, the productivity of American businesses has not been growing. In many instances, particularly in contrast to statistics for Japan and other foreign countries, productivity has been falling. This condition has been true for both profit-making and nonprofit organizations such as educational institutions.

For nearly all organizations and institutions, then, productivity goals must become formalized and improved to serve organizational goals. For this to happen, the available information technologies (data and word processing, telephone and mail services, and telecommunications) must be strategically planned, implemented, and integrated in all organizations during the 1980s.

Furthermore, says office systems consultant Amy Wohl, "It's crucial that you try out the new technology, or you're not learning to absorb it [Makower, 1981, p. 96]." Careful planning is important, but managers need to be wary of what Wohl calls "waiting until the market straightens itself out." Those who wait may find themselves facing technology so sophisticated that they have absolutely no understanding of how to get such systems to work.

Wohl also cautions against too much delay in the hope that prices will go down or technology will become more powerful. She tells executives who hold these views, "If you choose to stand with your head in the sand, you can be assured that your competitors will not do likewise. I come out of an economics background; there's something called 'comparative advantage': If your competitor chooses to use a business technique and you choose not to use it, you may be choosing to go out of business [Makower, 1981, p. 96]."

Word processing in particular, the technology with which many organizations begin, is changing dynamically and requires policy-level direction. At Indiana University, between 1978 and 1980, interest in word processing grew dramatically. More than 150 administrative and academic units expressed an interest in reallocating $1.8 million of existing budgets into the acquisition of word processing technology. At the same time the number of vendors who market word processing equipment and software also grew to more than 150.

From a narrow viewpoint, many vendors could satisfy word processing needs and increase individuals' productivity throughout the university. However, installing equipment from many vendors would seriously restrict our ability to (1) integrate word processing with other information technologies and (2) increase the overall productivity of individuals and the institution's cost effectiveness, not only in units that use word processors but in departments that train operators and maintain and repair equipment. These concerns hold for all organizations.

To increase the high probability of achieving technological integration, thereby achieving productivity goals, each organization must acquire its word processing hardware and software from vendors with architectural and technical specifications compatible with existing information technologies in other areas, especially data processing. Planners must also consider future needs for other capabilities (such as electronic mail, message switching, and graphics) that would use the same equipment. Finally, planners must consider ease of use and training of staff to use and maintain the word processing systems.

Keep as broad a view as possible. For instance, most managers think of electronic mail as something to be sent between offices in their company. Yet the day is not far off when telephone lines and "modems" ("black boxes" that translate electronic signals and help to send and receive them) will make it possible to communicate with any place that has a telephone, a modem, and receiving equipment. The technology already exists, but social and organizational practices haven't caught up to it.

OVERVIEW

Chapter 2 consists of parallel narratives of the same ordinary day in two offices—one with a modern office system and one without. These dialogues link traditional executive and clerical functions to their counterparts in the modern office. The purpose is to flesh out the processes hinted at in the vignettes and dialogues above. Chapter 3 describes the parts of a modern office system; in many ways it is simply a formal description of the processes described in Chapter 2.

Chapter 4 outlines the difficulties in trying to compare systems. Chapter 5 tells how to identify organizational needs and provides checklists for the job. Chapter 6, which tells how to find a high-quality technical solution, provides a study design, lists data sources, and suggests ways to summarize and evaluate data.

Chapter 7, which tells how to evaluate the needs of an office unit, also provides tools for the task. (Managers of small offices will probably want to combine the steps in Chapter 7 with the steps in Chapters 5 and 6.) Chapter 8 covers preparation for installation and training. Chapter 9 tells how to get extra benefits from your system. At the end is an annotated bibliography.

2 Two Snapshots: An Ordinary Day at the Office

This chapter describes two ordinary days in the office. The first section depicts work in a traditional office. The second part describes the same work in a modern office. You'll notice immediately the differences in technique. Look also for differences in work procedure, staff functions, amounts of work completed, accessibility of documents, and physical location of staff. Notice creative applications, such as putting phone messages into a message-switching system.

If you can't imagine what word wrap is, how electronic mail and message switching work, what automatic pagination looks like, or how a decimal tab behaves, this chapter is for you. If you've had experience with modern office equipment and are familiar with features like these, you'll probably prefer to skip this chapter and most of the next.

Sue Adams arrived just as the chimes announced that 9:00 A.M. had arrived. Stopping at the supervisor's office, she signed in and then headed for her office. The morning mail made a large, fat lump in the middle of her desk. She was just starting to open it when the

11

telephone rang. As she listened, she rummaged for a pencil and memo pad to take a message. After hanging up, she put the note on the corner of the desk, where Mr. Zellar always looked for messages. Returning to the mail, she discovered that in searching for a pencil, she'd managed to bury the letter opener and the piece of mail she was opening. Five more calls stopped her before she had finished with the mail. Checking her watch, she was amazed to find that it was already 9:35.

Her intercom buzzed; it was Mr. Zellar, ready to dictate. She grabbed her notepad and sharpened a fresh pencil. Then she arranged for Marge Anderson to intercept her calls because dictation always took a long time. Mr. Zellar never got his thoughts in order before dictating, so Adams spent many minutes sitting and waiting.

When she emerged, she had six long letters and 20 short ones in her notes. The short ones were identical, except that they were to go to 20 different people. She knew the letter by heart because she'd had to type the same letter 20 times last Monday, and 20 more the previous Monday.

She picked up the calls from Marge and then sat down to begin typing. She got out paper, carbon, onion skin, and an eraser. It still felt good not to have to get out the white paint—that hadn't been necessary since her correcting typewriter arrived several weeks ago. The only problem was, the lift-off ribbon corrected only the original, not the carbons. She still had to do those by hand.

Frowning at her notes for the first letter, she tried to guess how long it would be. Mr. Zellar wanted it on one page, but he also wanted margins as wide as possible. She supposed she'd have to type it at least twice before she got it just right. She moved the margin markers to the proper spots on the typewriter's guide ruler and set the paragraph tab. She was halfway through the letter when the telephone rang. She answered, put the caller on hold, buzzed Mr. Zellar, and then got back to the letter. Two more calls interrupted her before she finished the letter. It looked awfully crowded, but she decided to show it to Mr. Zellar before retyping it. Then, if he wanted to change anything else, she could make all the changes at the same time.

She started the next letter and was halfway through when she realized that her eye had skipped two lines—and the sentence she was typing didn't make any sense! Sighing, she pulled the paper from the typewriter and started over. This time she was nearly done before she made an error. She used the self-correcting ribbon on the original but had to erase the carbons by hand. She was glad she'd learned to put a curved metal ruler under the sheet she was erasing on. At least it prevented smudges on the carbons farther down. The telephone rang, making Adams put down the ruler and eraser. When she finished taking the message for Mr. Zellar, who was in conference, it took her a minute to find her place again.

She had just started back to work when Mr. Zellar buzzed; he wanted her to bring in coffee. When she finally finished the letter, she was tired. It was nearly lunchtime, and she knew that she made more mistakes just before lunch. She decided to do the rest after lunch. For now, she'd try to set up the conferences that Mr. Zellar wanted her to arrange. One involved nine people; the other, 12. He'd given her a list of times in order of preference. She called each person and reached the secretaries of all but one—a red-letter day! They would call back this afternoon with preferences. Then she'd eliminate the impossible times and try to get everyone to agree to the date that seemed the most popular. She hated to lean on people, but sometimes it was necessary, and Mr. Zellar was one of the firm's top executives. Most of all, she disliked the time this effort took. There had been days when she had spent an entire afternoon on the phone, just trying to get agreement on a date.

Lunch was a welcome break. Her friend Linda James had had the same kind of morning, and they sympathized with each other. After lunch Adams started the 20 form letters. They went slowly because the phone kept ringing, but at least they didn't require the concentration of the longer letters. When she made no errors and the telephone didn't ring, she could type one of the two-paragraph letters in just a few minutes, starting from when she began rolling the paper into the typewriter. It helped not to have to make carbons. She'd finally convinced Mr. Zellar that a copy of one letter and a copy of the list of addresses was all they needed for the file.

And speaking of filing, she'd better find time to do some. Her filing bin was overflowing onto the desk. Filing was tiresome now. The cabinets were crowded. Often she had to pull out the files and straighten them before she could put new material in. Then she had to put them back. Finding things in the files was just as much of a bother. She'd often wished that the files were cross-indexed. By 4:00 P.M. the 20 letters were done and the meetings had been arranged, so Adams started on the rest of the long letters. At 4:30 Mr. Zellar came out. He had written corrections on the letters and wanted them out before 5:00. He had also found typos in three of the form letters, but those could be corrected easily and could wait until morning. She started typing the first letter, hoping she wouldn't make any errors. She just had to get to the cleaner's before 5:30 or she'd have to wait another day for her winter coat.

Alex Zellar arrived at 8:00 A.M. He needed to finish the report on the Midwest Division. He also wanted to look over next year's budget *projections. The report lay on top of his in-basket, with several notes attached. Ms. Adams had found most of the missing information, but one set of tables was not yet available. She had contacted the computing center and learned that they would be ready Friday afternoon. He wrote a note requesting hand delivery of the tables as soon as they were ready and put the report back in his in-basket. He also wrote a note to Tim Bruce from Graphics, asking him to come in Friday afternoon for instructions on how to do the graphs.*

The budget figures were harder to find. They were near the bottom of the basket, and they, too, were awaiting a Friday morning computer run. Even so, the available figures showed that projected office staff costs were up again by 10%, but productivity didn't seem to be rising at all. He wondered to do about the problem. Hiring more staff didn't seem to help. In his own office, he had moved typing of long reports into the typing pool, but even that hadn't gotten his letters typed much faster.

He put the budget folder back in the in-basket and searched for the correspondence. He wanted it organized for dictation when Ms. Adams arrived. Near the top of the pile was the promotion letter and list. He had been sending out 20 each week—that seemed about all Ms. Adams could do without neglecting other work. Next, he scribbled several short notes and checked his calendar. He had a conference at 10:30, appointments all afternoon, and two meetings to schedule for next week. He also needed to set up the New York trip for the following week. As if that weren't enough, the dull ache in his lower jaw reminded him that he simply had to squeeze out an hour for a dental appointment.

Clearing his desk, he buzzed Ms. Adams for dictation. He had never liked doing it, but handwriting was worse. Once he'd tried to use a dictating machine, but no one had given him instructions, and he couldn't keep the buttons, strips, and disks straight. At least Ms. Adams sat quietly while he thought and didn't seem to mind how many times he had to try before getting some sentences just right. The only problem was, she couldn't type and take dictation at the same time.

When he'd finished dictating, he looked at the desk with satisfaction. Finally, he'd gotten something out of the in-basket! He returned several phone calls and then reached into his briefcase for the folder on the 11:00 conference. Striding down the hall, he noticed Marge Anderson dusting her desk. Didn't that woman have anything better to do? He realized that he couldn't recall ever seeing her at her typewriter. He'd have to speak to Ted Bates, whose secretary she was, about loaning some of her time to his office.

The conference carried over into lunch, where he mentioned the problem of rising office staff costs. The others were just as concerned. Jack Morgan, who was still new to the firm, mentioned an article he'd just been reading in Administrative Management, *on word processing and new ways to handle office work. Zellar wanted to explore the topic, but George Longman would have none of it.*

"Word processors are just expensive, special-purpose computers, and we don't need that just to type letters. All our secretaries have their own typewriters, and that's all they need. Besides, Alex, would you want to share Sue Adams with two or three other people? You keep her pretty busy as it is, and what would you do if you had a rush job and she was off doing something for someone else?" Alex had to admit that the prospect wasn't attractive. He was sure Longman's analysis wasn't correct, but he didn't know enough to respond. Perhaps he could read that article this evening.

After several hours of appointments, Zellar finally began reading and signing his mail. The form letters really got to him. He'd seen so many they all looked alike, and he found it hard to read for errors. It also irritated him when he found them. After the number she had typed, wouldn't you think Sue Adams could type them without errors? Now, come to think of it, wasn't form letters something word processing was supposed to be very good at?

He signed most of the letters, revised one, and took everything out to Ms. Adam's desk. He was sure that if they stayed a bit after 5:00, they could get out all but the form letters.

Fran Cook arrived just before 9:00 A.M. Before taking off her coat, she turned on the desktop display terminal, which looked rather like a small television set with a typewriter keyboard attached, and signed in. After hanging up her coat, she checked the small batch of mail beside the desk and sorted it into four piles: one for her and one for each of the managers for whom she provided administrative support services. Then she sat down at the terminal and started reading the messages. All of them were hers because her managers had their own desktop terminals and electronic "mail boxes." The first three items were the managers' list of tasks and priorities for the day. From these she created her own numbered list; then she erased the managers' memos.

The next item was a memo from Jody Lohman, supervisor of the word processing center, telling her that the 500 promotional form letters were done and would be brought over by courier before 9:30 this morning for Don Ragle to sign. Fran considered this production of form letters a marvel. Once the letter was correct, all the operator had to do was tell the system which mailing list to use, stack stationery in the sheet feeder, and start the run, which worked in "background" so that the operator could do other typing on the system while the letters were running. No errors could mar the letters because the system copied the same letter over and over. The only changes were the address, salutation, and certain coded words in the text.

The phone rang, interrupting her for a moment while she took a message, which she typed onto the terminal and "sent" to Don Ragle's "mailbox." Then she brought up other memos—Jeanne Pohl wanted to have lunch with her, Supplies notified her that the new stationery had arrived and would be up that afternoon, Publications had the mock-up of the new brochure for her to approve—could she check it about 11:00 that morning? The responses were quickly written and sent. The phone rang twice more before she finished reading; she typed the messages into the terminal just as she had the earlier ones.

One thing she liked about the electronic message system was the lack of mess on the desk. There was less mail because internal mail came through electronically. Telephone messages were easy to take and send. And answering electronic messages was easy. All she had to do was type Y (for YES) when the system asked whether she wanted to reply, and then type the message.

Even filing, once a nightmare, was now easy. To file a letter, all she had to do was type FILE. The system would ask, WHICH CABINET? and give a list from which she would choose one. Then it would ask, WHICH DRAWER? and give another list from which she would choose. Then, WHICH FOLDER? If she wished, she could cross-list the letter in other "files." When she or someone else searched, the letter could be identified by topic, addressee, writer, or date. Search and retrieval took only a moment or two—much less time than to search manually through crowded file drawers. Of course, the system's cabinets, drawers, and files weren't real in the metal-and-paper sense; they were electronic. However, the system's designer had organized them to work the same way office filing cabinets work.

One of Ragle's memos asked her to clean up a long letter he'd drafted. Still working on the same terminal, Cook typed WP to switch to the word processing mode, signed into their "port" with a password, and asked for the document with the name Ragle had given. She corrected several errors by typing correct characters over wrong ones, rewrote a few sentences, and then put the letter through the spelling checker. One small timesaver was the "word wrap" feature, which meant she didn't need to touch the carriage return to move from one line to the next. At the end of a line, if she was in the middle of the word, the processor simply moved the whole word to the next line. No more worry about typing too far into the right margin! She now used the carriage return only to end a line in a table, the last line of a paragraph, a heading, and the like.

Next, she turned on the dictaphone to rough out five more letters that Ragle had dictated. She was nearly finished when a blinking MESSAGE in the upper left-hand corner of her terminal told her that someone wanted her to check her mailbox right away. Finishing the letter, she switched to MAIL to discover that Ragle had finished the first letter and wanted it printed. And could she bring in a cup of coffee? She sent a message asking him to check the other letters, printed the first one, and then went for the coffee.

Returning to word processing mode, she started work for Dale Jamison, another of her managers, and began editing a project report for him. Still new to the firm, he often drafted on the word processor, but on long reports he still preferred to have a printed copy to edit by hand. She chuckled on reading the first few paragraphs. Jamison had copied them directly from the proposal for the project, written many months earlier, and they fit the context beautifully. Jamison was learning the shortcuts fast!

Halfway through one paragraph, she realized that she had overlooked a sentence, so she scrolled back in the text, pressed the INSERT key, and typed the missing sentence. When she finished the sentence, she pressed INSERT again to cancel the INSERT mode and scrolled forward to continue corrections.

When she was ready to insert the new table Jamison wanted, she pressed INSERT again. Then she set "decimal tabs" to help her line up the figures. After that, when she touched the tab key, the cursor moved to the spot where the decimal would print. As she typed the numbers, they moved toward the left margin until she typed the decimal. After it, the figures and the cursor moved to the right, just as if she were typing text.

The ease still surprised her. Until the word-processing system had been installed, she hadn't realized how much time she spent with correction fluid. In fact, she'd never had time for reports before — they had been done in the typing pool. Now, the operators in the word processing center, which had replaced the pool, frequently typed first drafts, but rarely was Fran Cook so busy that she didn't have time for corrections. Sometimes the managers made their own corrections because the electronic method was faster than writing with pencil. When she had finished, Cook sent the report to the laser printer in the word processing center. Then she went to Publications to check the brochure.

When she returned, the letters had been approved and were ready to print, so she turned on the printer. Not everyone had a printer in the office, but her section had so much rush correspondence that sending it to the WP center and waiting for a courier to deliver it delayed too many letters for too long.

While the letters were printing, she checked her mailbox and organized the afternoon's work: four draft letters to correct, six on dictation to draft, the Far West Division report and the budget statement to finish and put through the spelling checker—nothing unusual. In fact, she'd probably have time to work on the office procedures manual, which she had been revising to take into account the new office technology.

Don Ragle arrived at 8:30 A.M. and began work on the Far West Division Report. The Profit and Loss statement was in his mailbox. Don skimmed it, decided to include the last two tables in the report, and transmitted the document to the word processing system. Next were the budget projections. With satisfaction he noted that since June profits had been rising and the cost of support staff had been declining. So was the cost of paper. The new office technology had been installed in late April, and the actual savings so far were right in line with his expectations. Projections into the coming year showed additional savings.

Time to plan installations in all offices, Ragle mused. In their branch alone, the electronic mail and message switching were saving considerable time and money. With those capabilities spanning the country, the firm would save not only additional time but postage, telephone, and some travel money.

To show savings to date and projected savings, Ragle wanted some graphs, so he called up the graphics module and entered labels and data for each line. Beautiful! The program was so much more convenient than calling a draftsman. It even overstruck the trend lines to make them heavier than the axis lines. Ragle tinkered a bit until the graphs were just right. Then he typed in a title and added the graphs to the draft of the budget statement. Entering the message module, he asked Cook to print a draft of both reports and told the vice president that a draft of the budget statement would be on his desk this afternoon.

To set up the budget meeting, he typed in SCHEDULING. The terminal responded with, "What do you want to schedule?", to which Ragle responded "meeting on budget." "When?" "Wednesday, 2:30 P.M." "For how long?" "2.5 hours." "With whom?" Ragle listed nine names. For a few moments the terminal did nothing, although a small message in the corner informed him that it was CHECKING. Then a message printed out: "OK on all calendars. Shall I hold the time on all calendars? Y/N" Ragle typed Y. "Shall I send a note requesting the meeting? Y/N" Ragle typed Y.

For the meeting on the Far West Division, he went through the same process. The response this time was "Not OK. First free time, all calendars: Friday, 3:00 P.M. Shall I hold that time on all calendars? Y/N" Ragle typed "Y." "Shall I send a note requesting the meeting? Y/N." Here, Ragle reflected again, was another great timesaver. Cook and he sometimes had needed a day or more to set up large meetings. Ease of scheduling would be another advantage of installing modern office technology nationwide.

With the meetings set up, Ragle typed in a difficult letter and then sent Cook a message to clean it up and print it. He dictated most letters; with the hard ones, though, somehow he needed to see the words before him.

About that time the promotion letters arrived for signing. Ragle made a mental note to inquire about the price of an automatic signing device. With the rest of the process automated, hand signing something like this seemed unnecessary.

At 11:00 A.M. Ragle hooked up the teleconferencing equipment and dialed the New York office. It was time for his monthly meeting with the staff there. Among other advantages, the equipment enabled direct conversations, sharing of data and displays, and updates from computerized data bases when needed. Once the occasion for a tiring two- or three-day trip, these meetings now took very little time and fit nicely into the rhythm of his day. The conference ended shortly before noon.

The rumble in his stomach reminded Ragle that it was lunchtime. He headed to the employees' cafeteria for a quick sandwich. He had a meeting at 1:00, and he wanted a few quiet moments beforehand to prepare for it. At 3:00 he had a dentist appointment. At 4:00 he would be back for a file review with Bob Jones. One of the joys of office automation was that he could clear his desk daily without having to work several evenings each week.

One of the benefits to his firm was that he now had time for brief but regular meetings with all supervisees. It helped him keep on top of things, finding out about problems before they grew large. Often, too, he found the opposite—excellent work that deserved a reward. Twice, now, his routine meetings had turned up the fact that good employees were ready for advancement, and he'd been able to arrange promotion before they had gone looking for another job.

The Many Functions
3 Of Modern
Office Automation

This chapter describes the functions that can be performed by a modern office system—word processing, data processing, graphics, photocomposition, calendar keeping, scheduling, message switching, electronic mail, and teleconferencing. Electronic communication is the glue that coordinates these elements. Ultimately, large organizations will need all these features and will need to have them integrated under one communication system. Small organizations will choose some but probably not all of these functions.

The degree of integration and the balance of features will differ from one organization to the next and from one office unit to the next. For instance, a one-office business might not need electronic mail but might need photocomposition and graphics capability for brochures and other printed matter. A business with offices in several cities might not need photocomposition capability but would need electronic mail and message switching. Some businesses might have little need for word processing but great need for electronic mail and calendar keeping.

Read this chapter with your organization's work in mind. Which functions promise to reduce your workload substantially? Which could be installed in some offices but not others? Which could you do without now but want to install later? For instance, an organization that produces many long documents each having many revisions would save a great deal of time if it installed word processing. Calendar keeping and scheduling could save time each day for many secretaries and executives but probably not as much time as the word processor would. Photocomposition devices could help the publications department. An optical character reader (OCR) would enable any secretary to produce machine-readable copy on an ordinary electric typewriter, thus cutting the number of first drafts that have to be typed manually into the processor. One scanner could serve many secretaries, no matter where they were located.

Goldfield (1980a, p. 81) suggests thinking in terms of "backbone applications" of automation that could dramatically increase productivity. Typically, the backbone is word processing, which can increase the speed of text editing and manipulation two or three times over the speed achieved with typewriters. Depending on the amount of revision, the increase can be even greater. Once the backbone technology has been installed, additional technologies, such as scheduling, calendar keeping, and electronic mail, can be justified by the backbone application and added for little extra cost.

Modern office technology has been filtering into large organizations for some time now. In the 1980s, more and more of this technology will be moving into smaller offices. Where office computing was the most significant force for change in the 1960s and 1970s, office communications will probably be the most important force in the 1980s and 1990s. By the end of the 1980s, 30,000 of the largest offices will have an in-house telecommunications branch exchange (PABX) that electronically connects interoffice work—audio, data, and visual (Makower, 1980, p. 134).

Costs and data in the following examples are as of mid-1981. Because these facts change rapidly, don't take any detail as indicating how a system would perform in, say, 1985.

Sources of Information

There is no lack of reading material for those interested in office automation. Useful articles frequently appear in *Words,* published by the International Information/Word Processing Association (IWP); *Modern Office Procedures; Word Processing Systems; Output; Administrative Management; InfoSystems; Law Office Economics & Management; Management World; Office Equipment & Methods; Office Products; Technical Communication* (Journal of the Society for Technical Communication); *Word Processing Systems; Word Processing; Word Processing Report; Word Processing World; Datamation; The Office;* less specialized magazines such as in-flight and business magazines; and professional women's magazines such as *Savvy* and *Working Woman.* Everyone seems to be jumping on the office automation bandwagon.

In addition, membership in the IWP will bring you many useful booklets, surveys, studies, and bibliographies. Members also get a reduced rate at the IWP's frequent conferences. Books by Rosen and Fielden, McCabe and Popham, Stultz, and Waterhouse are listed in the bibliography. Several organizations—among them Datapro, Auerbach, and Seybold—put out regular reports on word processing and other office technologies. And some put on workshops that come with $500-plus price tags and Continuing Education Units (CEUs) for participants.

Still other sources of information are newsletters such as the IWP's *Viewpoint,* which is sent to all IWP members. In addition, *Computerworld* frequently carries articles on word processing.

To keep up with information on microcomputer-based processors, read magazines such as *Personal Computing, Popular Computing* (formerly *onComputing*), *Interface Age, Creative Computing,* and *Kilobaud Microcomputing.* It's a rare month that one of these magazines doesn't carry an article on one or more word processing software packages. Also read *InfoWorld,* which is the microcomputer field's equivalent of *Computerworld.*

As you read, look for organizations that seem like yours. What combinations of equipment did they use to meet their needs? Look also for ways to involve and interest staff members. When you finish a magazine or book, pass it along. The simple act of sharing information will involve some of your employees.

WORD PROCESSING

Word processing involves four processes—origination, production, reproduction, and distribution of documents. These processes occur in various ways, which are described below.

Origination of Documents

Words enter a system through typing (either of dictated text or text being composed by the typist), magnetic media (such as diskettes created earlier), electronic communication from another computer or processor, or optical character reading (OCR). Dictation and OCR require special equipment. Eventually, voice processing may eliminate the need to transcribe dictation.

Dictation systems.   Dictation is one of several ways in which words get into a word processing system. Dictation systems record data on either discrete media, such as cassettes or diskettes, or on endless loops inside central systems. The latter have the advantage that the typist, signaled by a light on a playback unit, can type along just behind the dictator.

Dictation equipment comes in desktop models, portable models, and central recording systems. Portable machines have the advantage of being able to be used nearly anywhere the user can carry them. However, most central systems can be accessed from telephones inside and outside an organization.

The importance of dictation is that (1) it takes up only one person's time and (2) it can be used whenever convenient for the dictator. Even so, office systems consultant Amy Wohl estimates that "between 10 and 15% of people who could use dictation equipment actually own some, and a smaller percentage actually use it" (quoted in Makower, 1980, p. 136). Even though dictation systems have been in many offices for years and may be installed in yours, don't take the system for granted. Consider its usefulness *in terms of* other office technologies. If your organization centralizes word processing in a center, chances are it will also need a centralized dictation system. If work stations are to be dispersed throughout the organization, desktop models may be more appropriate. Managers who travel a lot may prefer portable dictating machines.

Optical character readers (OCR). OCR input refers to the capability for direct connection between a word processing system and a scanner that can read printed or typed characters and convert them into digitized form as word processing documents. Some scanners will even read handmade correction marks. Optical scanning readers (OCRs), which used to require specially coded type fonts, can now read directly onto magnetic storage many kinds of text prepared on standard typewriters. This change means that first drafts no longer have to be prepared on a word processor. Instead, they can be typed on any ordinary typewriter, read onto the medium, and edited on the processor. The result is more word processing time for revising copy—the task that word processors do best.

Furthermore, optical scanners can (1) process data and information from various sources directly into Management Information Systems (MIS), (2) provide on-site transfer of previously stored data and information to assorted processing devices, and (3) integrate all sources of office data by providing a common input and output capability. Ultimately, technical advancements will produce OCR devices capable of reading paper of any color and even onionskin (Barber, 1980).

Projections are that during the 1980s, the OCR marketplace will double every three years, and equipment costs will decrease by half every three years. By the late 1980s, OCR devices will be available at a cost of about $1000, and vendors will have begun building OCR capability into the cabinets of word processors. In addition, OCRs will probably be able to read at a rate of 2,000 pages per hour. By that time, Barber (1980) muses, the cost of the box that holds the OCR capability may cost more than the internal electronics.

There are two product lines: (1) the intelligent, microprocessor-based unit that comes with software for applications such as communication, and (2) the dumb OCR unit with the intelligence to identify characters but no applications software. Prices range from $10,000 to $350,000.

Voice processing. Herbert Kaplan (1980) predicts that by the mid-1980s, voice processing will have advanced to the point that dictated text can be translated directly into printed form on an operator's display terminal. Indeed, voice processing is already available for computer systems (Speech Peripherals, 1981), although the technology is still fairly primitive.

Production of Documents

Traditionally, document production has occurred on typewriters. Now production technology has moved on through magnetic card or tape selectric typewriters (MC/STs and MT/STs) and electronic typewriters to display-based word processors with television-like screens. Most of these screens are based on cathode ray tube (CRT) technology.

Whatever system you choose, make sure that:

- The display supports a full assortment of characters, numbers, and symbols (a few systems support special symbols).
- The display characters are easy to read.
- The display is comfortable to view (so it won't cause operator fatigue).
- The display has operator control over brightness and contrast.
- The display face minimizes stray light reflection.

Remember, too, that displays range in size from a few characters or lines to a partial page, a full page (8½ by 11 inches) and even two full pages. Large displays usually cost more than small ones. For managers the important question is whether a given display size has a performance advantage for their applications.

In general, for firms that need several work stations, the best and most cost-efficient word processor will be some form of shared system. Some organizations, especially colleges, universities, and research institutes, will be best served by time-shared systems. For small firms the choice is generally between a stand-alone word processor and a microcomputer with word processing software.

Stand-alone word processors. Stand-alone word processors, designed for use by one person at a time, are self-contained units, often with a television-like screen, that allow users to store documents on magnetic media and then selectively retrieve all or portions of the documents for editing purposes.

Some of the more advanced stand-alone systems can establish a communications link with a computer and use high-speed computer printers instead of the slower, typewriter-like, "letter-quality" impact printers whose copy looks as if it had come from an ordinary typewriter. Costs range from $4000 to $8000 for systems with limited display and memory and from $8000 to $20,000 for systems with more memory, full video, and arithmetic (the ability to calculate columns in tables). Consider a stand-alone word processor if your firm has one or just a few offices. If you need communications, especially between offices, make sure the product you acquire can communicate.

Shared-logic word processors. Shared-logic word processors, designed to accommodate several users at the same time, share central control and memory circuits and work rather like interactive computer systems. Shared-logic means that word processing control and memory reside in a central computer and serve several work stations simultaneously. Shared-logic processors offer a wider range of peripherals such as printers and are generally more sophisticated than their stand-alone counterparts. A standard shared-logic processor has the following parts:

- A *central minicomputer* or microcomputer that contains the memory and controls all peripheral devices.
- Several television-like terminals (*CRTs*) with keyboards on which users enter and edit all documents.
- Several letter-quality *printers* and sometimes high-speed line printers.
- Magnetic *storage devices:* computer-compatible tapes, disk cartridges or packs, or diskettes.

Because most shared-logic systems can store a large number of documents, typists don't need to constantly shuffle media to find the specific document or document section desired. Elimination of the search time increases the amount of typing throughout.

Other features of shared-logic processors may include the following:

- The ability to receive input from optical scanner, communications link to a computer, or photocomposition interface.
- Compatibility with data processing terminals so that one terminal may be used for both data and word processing.
- User-programmable systems, which means that users can design very specific functions.
- The ability to link the processor with peripheral units that are located as much as 4000 feet away from it.

The cost of a shared-logic system ranges from $25,000 to more than $100,000. However, the cost per station is usually less than $12,000 and often offers an economic advantage over stand-alones when several stations are required. Furthermore, a shared-logic system usually offers more word processing features and functions.

The disadvantages of shared-logic systems include (1) the vulnerability of all work stations when part of the central system fails and (2) slower response from the system ("response time degradation") as more work stations are added to the system. The second problem appears in a system's slower response to keystrokes and in longer and longer printer queues. Systems from different vendors are described as supporting anything from two to twenty and more work stations. We found the vendors to be more optimistic than the equipment justified. Don't believe everything they tell you!

Protection from the first problem can include having two or more shared systems or a compatible stand-alone system so that rush jobs don't have to wait for a repair technician. Protection from the second requires planning conservatively and adding work stations and printers cautiously.

Consider a shared-logic word processing system if your firm is large enough to require several work stations and printers, especially if several will be required for a single building.

Distributed-logic word processors. Distributed-logic systems are much like shared-logic systems except that parts of the control and memory circuits are taken out of the central electronic package and put into the work stations. This design change reduces reliance on the central system, improves system response time, and reduces system degredation when additional work stations are added to a system.

Time-shared word processors. Time-shared word processing is based on large computer technology and is sometimes rented out to various customers. Input is done by means of a terminal connected to the computer, and output can be routed to a letter-quality printer. Traditionally, these systems have been designed more for data processors, including academics, than for secretaries, although researchers have been working to make them easier to use—"friendlier" (Ilson, 1980). One potential problem is slow response time when the computer is also a data processor and data processing is given priority. Researchers expect that within a few years, declining costs of the systems and of electronic printers, which make available an unlimited range of type styles and graphics, will put time-shared word processors within the financial reach of any organization that wants to use them.

Among the better-known systems are ATMS (an IBM product) and NROFF and RUNOFF. One of the newer systems, Scribe, designed for users who know little about document formatting, was developed at Carnegie-Mellon (Ilson, 1980). Another, Bravo, was designed at Xerox's Palo Alto Research Center and runs on Xerox's Alto computer. TEX (a computerized typesetting system) and METAFONT (a system for typeface design) were developed at nearby Stanford. TEX's outstanding ability to format complex equations led to its choice by the American Mathematical Society as the standard formatting language for manuscripts. At MIT, researchers have been building a prototype for Etude, which has many features similar to Bravo's.

The cost of a time-shared system ranges from $50,000 to more than $200,000. Cost per station is in the range of $7000 to $10,000.

Microcomputers. Microcomputer-based word processors, much like stand-alone processors, usually serve one person at a time. A system comes with a television-like screen, a central processor, diskette drives, and an operating system and word processing software on a floppy disk. The word processing software packages frequently offer more power and flexibility than a commercial stand-alone system even though the total package often costs less than a complete dedicated stand-alone. However, on-screen help for users, training manuals, and vendor support often are poorer than they are on the dedicated systems.

The combinations of hardware and software are nearly endless and ranged upward from about $4000 in 1981. Consider microcomputer-based word processing if yours is a small organization with one or a few offices and if you or someone in your firm has some knowledge of or aptitude for working with computers. Inquire about communication between offices and between types of equipment for both word processing and data processing. Have the secretarial staff try out any system you are considering seriously. Make sure the system you acquire has:

- At least 64K of on-line memory.
- At least two diskette drives.
- Most of the functions and features listed in Chapter 6.

By 1981 microcomputer-based word processors had become sophisticated enough that the IWP added a session on small business computers to its June 1981 Syntopicon.

Reproduction of Documents

Output can be produced and reproduced as hard copy (typed, printed, photocopied, microfiched) or electronic copy (on a diskette, disk, tape, or another user's screen—such as a memo typed and "sent" to someone else's electronic "in-basket"). When electronic copy is involved, one user's "output" becomes another user's "input."

Printers. Printers come in great variety. The daisywheel impact, letter-quality printer (named for its daisy-shaped printing element) has been joined by the thimble impact printer (named for its thimble-shaped printing element). Dual-element printers provide letter quality for two print elements at the same time. Impact printers are noisy unless they are housed in a sound-muffling case. Ink-jet printers, which are quieter, are useful for producing graphics and unusual printing such as Chinese characters. Ink-jet printing is now beginning to approach the quality of impact printers. Laser printers print much more rapidly than do the impact printers. They also enable one to print multiple character sets without the hassle of changing print elements. High-speed draft printers deliver copies much more rapidly than does an impact printer. The copy isn't of letter quality, but organizations that prepare long documents often prefer to trade quality for speed until a final draft is ready.

For managers, important points to consider are:

- How much letter quality copy does my firm produce?
- How much draft printing does my firm do?
- How much data processing and graphics printing does my firm do?
- How much use does my firm make of special character sets?

Intelligent copiers. When a system includes communication to intelligent copiers, typists can give the system typed instructions for photocopying the document directly from the electronic copy. They can even tell the machine how many copies to make and whether to collate and staple the copies. Makower (1980) predicts that copiers will gradually take on more and more of organizations' printing loads, using high-speed ink-jet and laser technology to produce large quantities of printed matter quickly. The availability of color will make this use of copiers even more attractive.

For managers, important points to consider are:

- How much copying is done of internally generated documents?
- Where are copiers located? Would automated, centralized copying save time and money?

Photocomposition. Photocomposition output refers to the capability for direct connection between a word processor and a phototypesetting unit. A photocomposition interface is especially important to organizations and departments that turn out printed material. At its simplest, the interface allows operators to transmit text from the word processor to the photocomposer (1) directly, through some form of communications system, (2) by media transfer, such as reading data from a magnetic diskette or tape into a computer, or (3) by OCR. Then a conversion program is used to strip off the word processing codes and insert the photocomposition codes. Some systems allow the WP operator to put in those codes before transmitting the text.

The major benefits are that operators keyboard the text just once and proofread it once. Thus, a letter-perfect word-processed text will produce a letter-perfect photocomposed text. However, the procedures are complex and not standardized. For managers, the important points are:

- How much of your work must be typeset (reports, brochures, sales material, and the like)? The greater the percentage, the more benefit you'll get from a photocomposition interface.
- Could you cut costs if you typeset more of your work? For example, one photocomposed page might contain text that required two typewritten pages. If your typed reports are long and have to be reproduced in many copies, typesetting them might save considerable money in paper, reproduction, and mailing costs.

Micrographics. Simply put, micrographics involves the use of computer output microfilm (COM) to store data (Cassin, 1981, p. 114), documents, and records, and computer-assisted retrieval (CAR) to retrieve it. Cassin argues that COM/CAR systems eventually will provide all large offices with low-cost accessible storage and retrieval of information. In his view, the day is coming when managers will not copy paper pages. Instead, they will choose to duplicate a single microfiche that holds anywhere from 98 to 260 pages each, in 10 seconds at a cost less than $0.10 per fiche!

For managers, important points to consider are:

- How much storage does your firm need and for what kinds of record?
- How accessible do the stored data need to be?

Reprographics. Although *reprographics* is simply the process of reproducing or duplicating documents, the term has come to be associated with modern reproduction techniques such as the use of automated typewriters, copying machines, high-speed duplicators, and phototypesetting equipment (Waterhouse, 1979, p. 144).

Important points for managers to consider include:

- The kind and quality of copying needed.
- The kinds of printers and duplicators that already exist.
- The organization of copying facilities—centralized or dispersed.

Data processing refers to the execution of a programmed sequence of operations on data through a programming language such as COBOL, BASIC, or FORTRAN. Many organizations want data processing capability built into their word processors. Like Don Ragle in Chapter 2, they want to be able to access company data bases, do analyses, and incorporate the resulting tables and graphs into their reports or turn them into displays for meeting presentations. Thus, the word processing terminal must be able to act as a data processing terminal, and the word processing software must be able to interact with data processing procedures.

This ability saves money and office space (one terminal does two jobs) unless an office has enough work of both kinds to keep two terminals busy all day long. It also prevents typing errors in tables and graphs.

At Indiana University, administrative data resided on an IBM 370/168 computer; research data were scattered among CDC, DEC, PRIME, and IBM 4341 computers. Thus, administrative users needed a word processing system whose terminals could mimic IBM 3780 data communications (so users could submit computer jobs to the IBM 370/168) and IBM 3270 communications ("CICS pass-through," thus enabling users of word-processing terminals to work directly with data). Academic users needed "asynchronous" work stations—that is, stations whose electronic communication code could be understood by the academic computers.

Kaplan (1980) predicts that by the mid-1980s, digital technology will have made possible sophisticated voice interactive and voice data-entry systems. Primitive systems are available now (Speech Peripherals, 1981), many of them to benefit print-handicapped users. Sophisticated voice systems will enable managers to enter data and examine files without knowing how to type.

For many firms data processing is the backbone technology. If data processing is not already installed in your business, plan for it when you plan for your other technologies.

GRAPHICS

Graphics capability enables operators to generate, display, and print line drawings, organization charts, bar graphs, pie charts, and other graphs from data supplied to the graphics package. Some word processing systems come with graphics packages, although these are not very sophisticated. Advanced graphics capability exists on many computers—another reason why word processors and computers should be planned to communicate with each other.

Interactive graphics—computer-aided design/computer-aided manufacturing (CAD/CAM)—was developed originally to help engineers and designers create standard engineering drawings (Cuozzo, 1981). Today, three-dimensional CAD/CAM systems enable users to:

- Create and update drawings.
- Protect original artwork and provide secure storage.
- Easily locate and retrieve existing illustrations.
- Interact with other functional areas of the organization.
- Reduce the tedium of repetitive tasks.
- Increase productivity.

Cuozzo (1981, p. G-10) points out that overall increases in productivity over manual methods range from 2:1 to 4:1. For individual tasks, the ratio can be as high as 20:1.

The typical work flow involves creating, retrieving, editing, storing, and merging with a text document (Cuozzo, 1981). Creation involves sketching with a digitizing stylus (or "pen"), specifying geometric coordinates, or copying and modifying an existing illustration—a process that is much like editing word-processed text.

For managers the important points are:

- How much does my firm use illustrations of any sort?
- If much use exists, what are the potential savings from installing a CAD/CAM system?

ORGANIZATIONAL AIDS

Many observers have noted that word processing and associated technologies have substantially increased the productivity of clerical activities. On the management end of business the gains have not yet been made. However, Goldfield (1980a, p. 135) sees increased professional productivity as an emerging priority because professional salaries account for 46% of total salary costs. Eventually, executives with terminals on their desks will use all the functions discussed in this chapter. However, most will probably start out by using some of the organizational aids described in the following paragraphs.

Calendar Keeping

Calendar keeping, as the name suggests, enables employees to keep their daily calendars on the system. The calendars are private— other users can't read a calendar that is not theirs. The calendar can't get lost or misplaced; pages can be printed if the user wishes; and they function just as a pocket calendar does, even providing reminders of birthdays, anniversaries, and the like, and serving as a tickler file.

Calendar keeping may not be worthwhile by itself. In conjunction with scheduling, though, it can be worth a great deal.

Scheduling

Scheduling is not possible without calendar keeping because scheduling uses the calendar to set up meetings. For instance, consider Alex Zellar's meetings. With a scheduling program, he could have asked for the computer system's scheduling module. The module would have asked him: "With whom?" He would have listed nine names for the first meeting and twelve for the second. The module would then have asked: "When (date and time)?" He would have specified his first choice, say, "06/10/02:30 P.M." Then he would have waited a moment while the computer checked the calendars of the listed individuals.

The computer would report back either "OK with everyone; shall I post the meeting tentatively and send a message requesting a meeting?" or "Not possible. First possible date is _____. Shall I post the meeting tentatively and send a message requesting the meeting?" If the latter, the manager could either type Y for Yes or request another date, in which case the computer would begin the search process again. At no time does the manager see the other parties' calendars; the computer does all the "looking" and matching. Such systems eliminate a great deal of work for both managers and support staff.

For managers, the important point to consider is:

- How much time do staff members spend scheduling meetings? The more time, the greater the savings from a scheduling module.

Message Switching

Message switching refers to the writing and sending of short memos and notes between work stations for display or printing. It enables users to send messages to one another through the computer or word processing system. The operation is similar to the process for sending a message that requests a meeting. The operator types a message and tells the system who on the system is to receive it. When someone "opens" the message by calling it up on his or her screen, the system asks whether the recipient wants to send a reply. One company found the system so easy to use that message originators were getting responses that said, simply, "Yes," "No," "Tuesday's fine," and other such cryptic statements! Without the context of the original request, the response made no sense. To cope with the problem, that company programmed the message system to attach the first three lines of any memo to the recipient's response.

Message switching saves a great deal of executive and support staff time. Brief memos are much easier to type into a terminal than to draft on paper and hand to a secretary, who then has to type it and bring it back for checking and signing. Furthermore, Kaplan (1980) predicts that by the late 1980s, some vendors will be offering voice message and reminder systems, which will enable nontyping executives to use terminals as easily as anyone else.

Both message switching and electronic mail (see next section) make it possible to send a message as rapidly as it can travel over a telephone line or by a satellite connection. The addressee can read the message right away, if he or she happens to be on the system when the message is sent, or at a later time.

Makower (1980) argues that the sheer increase in speed of communication will change the way managers and executives spend their time. In our study we found some evidence of change in a firm that had installed terminals on both executives' and secretaries' desks. Our observer had noticed that more and more secretaries were doing forecasting and other routine computing tasks that required only typing in certain numbers when the computer asked for them. The executives, meanwhile, were drafting and sending their own memos and generally keeping in much closer touch with staff and with each other. At least in this case, automation appears to have freed the executives to become better managers.

Electronic Mail

Electronic mail enables operators to write and send letters and documents, including "carbon copies," through an electronic communications system, a faster and sometimes cheaper process than using paper mail. Recipients can either print the documents or display them on a screen. Many organizations begin by using this capability for local, internal documents, but in large organizations, electronic networks already pass documents back and forth not only throughout the United States but overseas. Some electronic mail originates on and prints at telex and TWX machines that resemble typewriters but have an additional telephone dial located on the keyboard. Some electronic mail originates on and prints at facsimile machines, which can transmit anything that can be placed on paper. Some, such as Western Union Mailgrams, travel by computer. Networks such as Telenet enable scholars and researchers to send copies of their documents to as many others on the network as they wish.

For managers, important points to consider are:

- How large is the flow of documents between offices?
- What are the current costs of transmitting documents?
- How rapidly do documents need to travel?

TELECONFERENCING

Teleconferencing makes possible meetings between individuals who are thousands of miles apart. Today, users of teleconferencing systems do so with the help of communicating business information systems and electronic blackboards. A portable system allows hard-copy conferencing from any telephone. Recently, according to Goldfield (1980a), new techniques have added visual capability that permits a sense of

> full verbal communication with the ability to watch facial expressions and body language for cues; it also allows the addition of data, documents, image and drawing displays with still-frame and slow-scan video augmentation. . . . Changes in data and decisions reached during a meeting can be incorporated into the firm's data base, updating old information and providing a permanent meeting record [p. 141].

Firms without teleconferencing equipment can gather in a central location that provides the necessary equipment (one major hotel chain presently makes such facilities available). Eventually, most offices will routinely contain the equipment, thus making possible meetings among participants in many locations.

The potential savings in executive time are staggering. Many meetings are a waste of time, yet the traveling to get to those meetings usually takes much more time than the meeting, and, of course, the travel is necessary for all meetings, productive or not. Increasingly, executives who use teleconferencing will be able to save substantial amounts of travel time alone. In addition, they won't suffer from jet lag and work loss caused by travel.

For managers, important points to consider include the number of meetings scheduled, the parties and organizations involved, and their physical locations.

TELECOMMUNICATIONS

Telecommunications glue systems together—word and data processing, graphics, photocomposition, calendar keeping, scheduling, message switching, electronic mail, and so forth. The requirements for successful communication are highly technical—easily the subject of an entire book.

For managers, the important points are:

- Identify the communication codes your existing equipment uses.
- Find out which vendors have systems that can interface with yours.
- Insist on a test to demonstrate the alleged capability. (For more details, see Chapters 6 and 7.)

Even a small firm with a single microcomputer for both data and word processing needs to consider this question. Word processing packages exist that will interact with data processing files, and some microcomputers can telecommunicate.

4

The Problem: Apples + Oranges + Grapes = Fruit Salad

Standardization has not yet affected office automation. The purpose of this chapter is to alert managers to the differences and potential problems. Every system has one or more features that are awkward to the point of near impossibility for daily use. Sometimes the presence of a feature is important for some uses and not others. For instance, most businesses wouldn't need on-screen Greek, math, and equations, but most academic and research institutes would.

Consider six major criteria when you evaluate office automation products:

- Architectural and technical specifications.
- Word processing features and functions.
- Other features and functions.
- Ease of learning.
- Vendor service and support.
- Cost.

Within each of these categories is a list of specific items (see Tables 4.1-4.2) that shoppers for automation products can treat as a checklist. The relative importance of these criteria and items will vary from one organization to the next. The lists in Tables 4.1 and 4.2 are extensive but not necessarily exhaustive. When you use them, ask your staff to help you make them complete for your purposes. For instance, on architectural and technical specifications, managers of firms with computers should consult with their computing staff and other technical personnel, who will adjust the lists to meet the requirements of the firm's computing technology.

ARCHITECTURAL AND TECHNICAL SPECIFICATIONS

Architectural and technical specifications describe hardware, software, communications, printing, document storage, and terminal characteristics. View these specifications from the perspective of function, not hardware per se. Do you need conferencing capability? Information retrieval to speed research? Information and document transfer? Word and data processing by individuals with desktop terminals? Do you need assistance with managing activity—automated reminders, tickler files, project management scheduling, itinerary planning, and so forth?

Having answered these questions, look for overlap between functions. For instance, Goldfield (1981a) points out, information retrieval and transfer are closely related, as are individual processing and activity management. Thus the equipment that serves one function might also serve another. At this point managers can relate the functions they need to the IPSOD acronym mentioned earlier—what do they need for **i**nput, **p**rocessing, **s**torage, **o**utput, and **d**istribution (Goldfield calls the last item "transport").

To give a specific example, at IU we wanted terminals that would handle both word and data processing. Thus, for administrative word processing, one of our technical requirements was terminals with bisynchronous communication because that's what our administrative computer understood. For academic word processing, we required terminals with asynchronous communication because that is what our academic computers required. By the way, managers don't need to know the technical details of terms like these, but they *do* need to know that the technical requirement exists.

You will probably want to require software-based word processors so that improvements can be made simply by changing a diskette or mounting a tape with the new software. If the word processing capability were "hardwired" into the equipment, as part of the hardware, any change would require purchasing new hardware. For stand-alone word processors, you might want to require that the processor be (1) upgradable to a system with more than one work station and/or (2) capable of communication.

Table 4.1 Characteristics of Word Processing Systems

Features	Product Being Evaluated:[a] Vendor A, XYZ Processor
Architectural and Technical Specifications	
Hardware Devices	
Flexible Mix Between Printer/CRTs	_____
Stand-Alone Expands	_____
Stand-Alone Communicates	_____
Cable Distance: Minimum ___ ft.	_____
Foreground/Background Operation	_____
Communication Speed: ___ BAUD	_____
Computer Interface	_____
RJE 3780 Emulation	_____
CICS/3270 Protocol	_____
Optimum Number of Devices	_____
Digitized Voice Processing	_____
Printing	
Queuing	_____
Twin Track	_____
Wide Track	_____
Draft Speed	_____
Cut Sheet Feeder	_____
Envelope Feeder	_____
Document Storage	
Hard Disc Capability—Minimum ___ MB	_____
Expandable Disk	_____
Floppy Disk Capacity	_____
Terminals	
Full-Page Display	_____
Partial-Page Display	_____
Local Intelligence	_____
Detachable Keyboard	_____
Tilt Screen	_____
Magnification	_____
Word Processing Features and Functions	
Display	
Scrolling	
Horizontal	_____
Vertical	_____
Exact image of print	_____
Sub- and superscripts	_____

Table 4.1 Characteristics of Word Processing Systems (Cont.)

Features	*Product Being Evaluated:[a]* *Vendor A, XYZ Processor*
Word Processing Features and Functions	
Control code display	_____
Greek and Math	_____
Multicolumn	
Associated	_____
Snaked	_____
Format statement	_____
Automatic Features	
Word Wrap	_____
Margin Adjust	_____
Decimal Tab	_____
Input Underline	_____
Centering	_____
Boldface	_____
Line Spacing	_____
Page Numbering	_____
Pagination	_____
Repagination	_____
Header/Footer	_____
Widow Line Adjust	_____
Footnote Control	_____
Miscellaneous	
Stored Words/Phrases	_____
Mailing List/Merge	_____
Multicolumn	_____
Forms Fill-in	_____
Revision Marking	_____
System Security	_____
Scientific Equations	_____
Records Management	_____
Table of Contents Generation	_____
List of Tables, Illustrations	_____
Index Generation	_____
Access to Other Documents	_____
Temporary Margin	_____
Hyphenation Help	_____
Document Assembly/Merge	_____
Search	_____
Selective Search/Replace	_____

Table 4 1   Characteristics of Word Processing Systems (Cont.)

Features	Product Being Evaluated:[a] Vendor A, XYZ Processor
Word Processing Features and Functions	
Global Search/Replace	_____
Block Move/Copy	_____
Column Move/Delete	_____
Sort, Alphanumeric	_____
Spelling Dictionary	_____
Proportional Print	_____
Justification	_____
Math	_____
Other Capabilities of Modern Office Technology	
Data Processing	_____
Electronic Mail	_____
Message Switch	_____
Graphics	_____
Scheduling	_____
OCR Input	_____
Photocomposition Output	_____
Intelligent Copier	_____
Micrographics	_____
Ease of Learning	
Classes for Trainers	_____
Classes for Users	_____
Self-Paced Training Package	_____
(Customer's site)	_____
National Hotline (800)	_____
User Groups	_____
User or Vendor Newsletter	_____
User Reference Materials	_____
Built-in System Aids	_____
On-screen menus	_____
Help command	_____
On-screen prompts	_____
Turn off or bypass menus/prompts	_____
Support and Service	
Office Systems Consultant Support	
Site preparation	_____
Problem solving	_____
Application support	_____

Table 4.1   Characteristics of Word Processing Systems (Cont.)

Features	Product Being Evaluated:[a] Vendor A, XYZ Processor
Support and Service	
Systems analysts	_____
Maintenance service	_____
Availability of maintenance service	_____
New product announcements	_____
Purchasing Support	
Pricing changes	_____
Sales representative response	_____
Billing support	_____
Supplies	_____

[a]Use one checklist per product. Fill in vendor's name below "Product Being Evaluated." Chapter 6 tells how to evaluate each feature and fill in the blanks to reflect that evaluation.

For most large organizations, the most important criterion will be architectural and technical specifications because computers and a computing network are already in place and working. It would not be cost-effective to replace the computers and the network solely because planners want to buy a word processing system that can't communicate with them.

Mary Smith asked six different vendors of shared systems, "Will your word processing terminal communicate with my XYZ computer? Will I be able to submit computer jobs and work with data online?"

All six replied, "Yes." Sounds simple, but Smith, alerted to the lack of standardization, probed for more details and found the following:

- *One vendor's equipment provided these capabilities for only one terminal at a time, and only on a dedicated telephone line. Furthermore, the terminal had to have stand-alone capability.*
- *Another provided both capabilities, but only if the buyer acquired additional expensive equipment from another vendor. Furthermore, use of the equipment would be awkward.*
- *One vendor didn't yet have working ability to do data processing online. It was a future capability that the vendor had been hoping to have ready by the time an order was placed. He hadn't expected to be asked for an actual test.*
- *The rest provided both capabilities from any terminal.*

Table 4.2 Cost of Word Processing System[a]

Vendor	Rank	No. of Processors	Total $ Hardware	Total $[b] Software	$ Sub Total	4 Years Mainten.	$ Tot.
Vendor 1							
Vendor 2							
Vendor 3							
Vendor 4							
Vendor 5							
Vendor 6							

[a] Vendors bid on a system to include ____ terminals and ____ printers.
[b] Include purchase price and annual charges for ____-year period.

The following sections list architectural and technical specifications by category and define the terms as we use them.

Hardware Devices and Communications

A *flexible mix between printers and work stations* means that of the total number of printers and work stations that can be attached to a system, the ratio of printers to work stations is not fixed. Some systems require, say, one printer for every two stations. Some organizations need that ratio. Other organizations may need one or even two printers per station, depending on the amount of revising done and the length of documents. The more revising and the longer the documents, the greater the need for printers.

Minimum cable distance refers to the longest distance cables have to reach between the central processor and the most distant work station and other peripheral devices. For instance, if the most distant device will be 2000 feet from the central processor, you'll have the rule out systems whose maximum distance is less than that.

Foreground/background operations refer to whether a system can provide operations such as communications, merge, print, global search and replace, and the like simultaneously with other operations. With foreground/background operation, an operator can, for instance, set up a form letter to merge with addresses in a mailing list, stack paper in a printer, start the operation, and then work on another document while the letters are printing.

Communication speed refers to the rate at which information passes from one part of a system to another. For instance, you might want to require that the system and its devices be able to communicate at 4800 BAUD (i.e., bits per second—BPS—or about 500 characters per second—CPS) and that the system and a host computer be able to communicate at 9600 baud or greater.

Computer interfaces depend on what computers your firm wants the word processor to communicate with.

42

RJE 3780 emulation refers to the ability to communicate with computers or with other systems that use IBM 3780 data communication terminals to communicate with the computers. Put differently, the terminals on the word processor must be able to mimic the 3780 terminal.

CICS/3270 protocol refers the ability to make an IBM computer think that it is talking to an IBM 3270 information display system.

The *optimum number of devices* will vary from firm to firm. In our case, campus layout dictated that systems with central or master processors should support at least 24 devices per processor for administrative users and 60 devices per processor for academic users. We lowered by 25% the vendors' estimates about the number of devices supported because we believed the estimates to be too optimistic, and we didn't want overloads to degrade performance.

Digitized voice processing converts spoken words into digital signals that can be transmitted, decoded, and stored for retrieval elsewhere. This system, with the aid of a computer, is the voice version of electronic mail. The technology, still quite new, is very expensive.

Printers

Queuing refers to a system's ability to allow several documents to be lined up, or queued, for subsequent printout while the operator works on other tasks. Queueing should include the ability to delete documents from the queue and/or to print priority documents ahead of others in a normal first-in first-out queue.

A *twin-track* printer is a letter-quality printer with two print elements to allow printing of two different fonts in the same line at the same time. This capability is important when documents contain Greek or other nonroman letters or mathematical symbols.

A *wide track* letter-quality printer has a carriage wider than 15 inches and can print line lengths up to 254 characters.

Draft speed is 120 CPS or more. To date, draft printers have not been able to match the quality produced by impact, letter-quality printers.

A *cut sheet feeder* is an attachment to a letter-quality printer that feeds sheets of paper without operator intervention. Some models allow for both letterhead and second-sheet paper.

An *envelope feeder* attaches to a letter-quality printer and feeds standard envelopes without operator intervention.

A *sound controller* is a sound-muffling case that holds a printer, including sheet feeders. A sound controller keeps the sound of an impact printer at an acceptable level. This feature is important because recent research has shown that constant noise, even at levels supposedly nondangerous to hearing, makes people nervous and irritable.

Hard disk capability—minimum number of megabytes refers to high-capacity, random access, magnetic storage media. Disks may be nonremovable. Find out the average amount of storage space needed by each proposed terminal and printer on the system. Multiply the average by the total number of printers and terminals.

An *expandable disk* refers to a system's ability to accept more disk drives as storage needs grow beyond the system's initial capacity.

A *floppy disk* is an 8-inch or 5¼-inch circle of mylar coated with a magnetic material and enclosed in a protective envelope that holds 30 or more pages of text. Unlike cassettes or cartridges, which store text serially, diskettes are formatted in a random manner that allows faster access.

Terminals

Full page display refers to the work station's ability to show at least 65 lines of text, or a whole page (8½ by 11 inches) at one time.

Partial page display refers to the work station's ability to show at least 20 lines of text from a page at one time.

Line display refers to the work station's ability to show only a line of text at a time.

Local intelligence refers to the presence of a microprocessor in the terminal to permit most editing activity to take place at the terminal. This capability is important because it minimizes activity at the master processor.

A *detachable keyboard* is a design characteristic of the work station that enables the operator to move the keyboard independently from the display.

A *tilt screen* is a design characteristic of the work station that enables the operator to change the angle of the screen to reduce glare or otherwise increase personal comfort.

Magnification is a feature of some display screens that enables the operator to choose between a full page of text at regular character size or a half page at double (vertical) size.

WORD PROCESSING FEATURES AND FUNCTIONS

Features and functions refers to the various WP display and automatic features that affect the operator's ability to manipulate text. This section lists and defines important word processing features and functions. You will notice some overlap because many of the functions and features depend on one another.

Scrolling allows access to text that will not fit on a video display screen for review or editing. *Horizontal scrolling* is the ability to move horizontally along a line of text to access more characters than may be shown on the screen at one time. Several methods exist. Some systems move lines of text horizontally, adding one character at a time; others display the text as overlapping left, center, and right segments. Still others display wide lines by reducing character size, thereby showing more characters at the same time than is possible with regular size. *Vertical scrolling* is the ability to move up and down through the text, a line at a time. To the user, the text appears as a continuous stream like a scroll, rolling off a holder at one end and onto a holder at the other.

Exact image of print refers to the ability of the screen on a work station to show true proportionally spaced and justified text with bold characters, underlines, sub- and superscripts, and so forth, just as the text will print.

Sub- and superscripts refers to the ability of the screen to display characters a fractional increment (sometimes adjustable) above and below the line for footnotes, formulas, and the like.

Control code display refers to the ability of a system to display instructions, commands, or codes on the work station screen. In some systems the operator may choose between displaying text with codes, or only the text as it will appear on printout.

Greek and math refers to the ability to facilitate technical typing and equation typing by not only printing a Greek-letter or math-symbol character set simultaneously with another character set but also by displaying the letters and symbols on the work station's screen. Some systems help this ability by enabling operators to turn off word wrap, by quarter spacing for super- and subscripts, and by defining equation zones that preserve character placement. In 1981, most systems lacked on-screen Greek and math.

Multicolumn format refers to the ability to display text or numerics in multiple columns during editing. Columns can be either associated pairs, as when an item in one column is associated with an item in another, or "snaked," like magazine columns, so that text flows from the bottom of the left-hand column to the top of the right. Some systems also enable typists to "swap" columns as easily as they can transpose two letters that have been typed in the wrong order. This feature is especially useful in tables.

Many systems display a *format statement* with every screenful of text. Operators set or change the format statement whenever they want to set or change margins, tabs, and spacing. Most systems allow operators to change these features at will throughout a document. Furthermore, most processors allow the format to be changed at any time during document preparation. Thus, typists may use triple spacing and wide margins on drafts even though they will use single spacing and narrower margins on the final copy.

Automatic Features

Word wrap automatically moves a word from one line to the next if it does not fit on the line being typed. Word wrap also means that a system can wrap words while adjusting margins. With the wraparound feature, typists never have to type a carriage return (except at the end of a paragraph, heading, or otherwise fixed line ending) because a new line starts automatically each time the cursor reaches the right margin. When the cursor reaches the margin in the middle of a word, the whole word moves to the next line.

Margin adjust means that operators can change margins with a single command, automatically changing line endings without further intervention. The change can affect either an entire document or just a small section, such as a quotation.

A *decimal tab* automatically aligns columns of decimal figures on the decimal point. The typist simply tabs to a column and types numbers without regard for alignment.

Input underline means that an operator can indicate the beginning and end of underlining with a code or key, in which case the text underlines automatically as the operator types. This saves backspacing and underlining character by character. Some systems allow the operator to choose between underlining words only or spaces and words.

Centering means that a word processor automatically centers a word or text segment. This function usually works by a keystroke(s) that tells the system to center the previously typed or the next text segment between the margins. A few text formatters use a command instead. For instance, centering a line might require typing, say, "/CTR/Heading". The text won't center on the screen but *will* center on the typed page.

Boldface capability means that the system can print specified portions of text in a darker intensity than the rest of the text. Boldface highlights titles and headings and emphasizes words and phrases. Ease of use varies dramatically from one system to the next. For instance, on one time-shared system, use of the boldface feature requires the operator to strike three keys for *each* single overstrike on each single character. Thus, to boldface "to," the operator would have to strike keys eight times—one time for each character and three times per character for the overstrike. Under such circumstances, most operators would choose to avoid boldface, even if it would enhance the appearance of a document. In contrast, most systems allow the operator to turn boldface on and off with a key or command. Thus, the operator merely strikes the key, types the word or words, and then strikes the key again.

Line spacing enables different line spacings (single, double, triple, etc.) within the same document without physically changing settings on the printer when the document is printed ("played out").

Page numbering means that the word processing systems can automatically generate page numbers within documents. *Pagination* is the ability to divide a multipage document into pages of a specified number of lines. This feature is often joined with the automatic generation of page numbers. *Repagination* automatically changes page endings when text is inserted or deleted within a document, or when a new page length is desired. The system breaks the text into pages of the desired length and renumbers them correctly. Some systems allow operators to reject specific page breaks. For instance, one popular system paginates on the screen in response to a command key. The screen highlights the text through the last line that would appear on a page. If the operator likes the break, he or she says "ok" by pressing the EXECUTE key. Otherwise, the operator uses an "arrow" key to move the page break a line or two higher or lower before pressing EXECUTE. See also *widow line adjust.*

Header/footer capability means that the system will place header/footer text at the top or bottom of each page of a multipage document. The operator specifies the text once, and the header/ footer is automatically added during printout. Operators can change the main document text without affecting the headers and footers.

Widow line adjust prevents a title, a heading, or the first line of a paragraph from being the last line on a page. It may also prevent a last line from being the first line on a new page. This feature is especially desirable when paging or repaging is automatic.

Footnote control ties a footnote to the piece of text it goes with. If the text segment is moved to another page or document, the footnote travels with it. This feature isn't needed in ordinary office typing, but it is a boon in academic and other technical typing.

Mailing list/merge means that the system can create and maintain mailing lists that can be used over and over again, sorted by different characteristics, and merged with letter text for personalized mass mailings.

Forms fill-in is the ability of a system to facilitate fill-in typing on preprinted forms. This process works by filling in the blank spaces, known as fields, and automatically skipping from field to field in response to a carriage return or some other single action.

Revision marking refers to automatic marking of places in a document where the writer has inserted, deleted, or changed portions of text. The revision mark is usually a vertical bar typed in the left-hand margin.

System security refers to a requirement that the operator key in a confidential password code before the system itself or, alternatively, specific documents can be viewed or revised.

The capability for *scientific equations* facilitates the entry and editing of equations by means of features such as quarter-line spacing, turning off word wrap, and defining equation zones to retain character placement.

Records management refers to the ability to create and maintain files of information that can be manipulated in various ways, for instance, to select from certain fields, to resequence, and to generate lists.

The *generation of table of contents* is a feature that scans a document and prepares a table of contents, using section and paragraph headings in the document and the page numbers on which they are found. Should a later revision change the page numbers and order of topics, the operator need only ask for a new table of contents. For long documents such as proposals, computer documentation, reports, and books, this feature saves writers and operators substantial amounts of time. Furthermore, because the entries come directly from the text, there is no chance for a typing error that isn't also in the text.

Automatic lists of tables and illustrations refers to the system's ability to scan a document and prepare lists of tables and lists of illustrations from their titles and captions.

Index generation is a feature that scans a document and prepares an index using coded words and phrases in the text. The index is alphabetized, and each entry lists all page numbers on which the entry appears.

Stored words and phrases refers to the storage and reuse of text. Most typed material contains some words and phrases that are frequently repeated. For instance, in Chapter 3, we often use the terms "shared-logic" and "stand-alone." To save typing these terms completely every time, we stored the words with two code letters that would reproduce the full phrase with every typing of the code letters. Different companies refer to the stored phrases variously as "macros," "variables," "glossary entries," or "stored phrases." Some systems allow storage of up to a page of text with each entry. As Chapter 9 shows, this feature can greatly increase the speed of document preparation. It can also ensure consistent usage of technical terms.

Access to other documents refers to a system's ability to allow operators to enter and copy parts of existing documents for use in a new one. As Chapter 9 shows, this feature can greatly increase the speed of document creation.

Temporary margin means that a system can set a second, different margin for purposes such as indented paragraphs and extracts.

Hyphenation help refers to techniques that the system uses to hyphenate words. One such option, "hot zone hyphenation," requires that any word that enters but does not fit within a predefined end-of-line space must be either manually hyphenated or moved to the next line. Another option scans through the text and stops at any place where a hyphenation decision is required. More sophisticated systems may use an algorithm (i.e., formula) to make these decisions, or they may store a dictionary of hyphenations and hyphenate automatically.

Document assembly/merge refers to the way in which a system can assemble new documents from previously recorded text. Most systems can combine prerecorded text with keyboarded text. Many systems can combine selections from prerecorded text to form a new document. Document assembly/merge also describes a system's ability to join a document to variable information (such as names and addresses) to create many nearly identical documents.

Search capability automatically locates a string of characters and displays it on the work station's screen.

Selective search and replace is the ability to search for the occurrence of a character string so that an operator can either delete or change it.

Global search/replace refers to the ability of a system to search for repeated occurrences of a character string (typically of up to 32, 64, or 128 characters long). The system can then automatically replace one string with another, either one at a time or all at once, depending on the operator's preference. For instance, suppose the word "accommodate" were misspelled "accomodate" throughout this chapter. We could correct all these errors with a single search-and-replace sequence. (One of the processors will even tell you how many times it had to correct the mistake!) Global search and replace is especially useful with form letters and paragraphs of text that are used over and over again.

Block move, copy, and delete are closely related. *Block move* is the electronic equivalent of cutting pages up and taping them together in a new order, either within a document or between documents. The operator marks the beginning and the end of the block and then marks the spot to which the block is to be moved. The lines of text move together to close the gap left by moving the text. Similarly, the lines of text open up to receive a block that is moved into existing text. *Block copying* is much the same except that the block of text stays where it is and one or more copies show up in whatever locations the operator designates. *Block delete* involves marking a block and taking it out without moving it anywhere.

Column move/delete is the ability to manipulate characters vertically within a column. For instance, you might want to swap the positions of two columns in a table. This feature is important for tabular work because a column can be moved or deleted with a minimum number of commands. In less sophisticated systems, columns must be moved or deleted a line segment at a time, in multiple steps.

Sort, alphanumeric refers to a feature that can sort files, arranging them in alphabetical, numerical, or some other order.

This feature is important on systems that sort or manipulate address lists. It also permits changes to be entered randomly.

A *spelling dictionary* locates misspelled words in a document and highlights the words for verification and possible correction. This function usually uses a vendor-supplied dictionary with the customer having the capability to add or delete words.

Proportional spacing. See *Justification,* below.

Proportional print refers to typed, printed, or displayed text where each alphanumeric character is given a weighted amount of space. For instance, an "i" might be two units wide, an "L" four units wide, and a "W" five units wide. Such printing has a typeset appearance, especially when combined with additional adjustments (called "kerning") between specific pairs of characters, such as "T" and "r", so that the "r" rests mostly under the bar of the "T".

Justification is the ability to produce printout with an even right-hand margin. This result may be achieved by interword spacing (i.e., leaving extra white space between words) or by intercharacter spacing with proportionally spaced characters, both of which give the output a more typeset appearance.

Math or *math pack* refers to the capability of the system to do mathematical calculations on columns and rows of numbers contained in a word processing document.

OTHER CAPABILITIES

Many organizations will view word processing as a starting point in the development of an integrated office system that contains several elements. As the narratives in Chapter 2 show, electronic mail and message switching, which move text from point to point or from person to person electronically, save time and costs in the distribution of information. Electronic calendaring and scheduling can also improve operations throughout an organization. Optical character recognition (OCR) input enables offices to create word processing files from typewritten text. Micrographics allows highly reduced copies of documents to be indexed for later retrieval and review. These and other capabilities should be available either as options or as improvements planned by the vendor for the near future. Chapter 3 discusses these options in more detail.

EASE OF LEARNING

Ease of learning refers to the ease with which operators can learn to use the system. For instance, some vendors provide training mainly through a self-paced training package that comes with each work station. The package usually includes a workbook, reference guide, manual, and audio cassettes. Also important are on-screen menus and prompts, ability to turn off menus and prompts, and transferability of experience on a stand-alone word processor to a shared-logic system by the same vendor. Some vendors make a direct charge for the initial training and any later training provided.

Ease of learning is important if (1) your firm plans to provide its own training and user support and/or (2) your firm has a high rate of turnover among clerical employees. Organizations that plan to let the vendor do all training and/or that have low turnover might pay less attention to ease of learning.

The following paragraphs list and define some of the features that affect ease of learning:

Classes for trainers refers to whether a vendor offers classes that would teach an organization's staff how to train its own operators.

Classes for users refers to whether a vendor offers classes to train operators. These classes can take place in either the vendor's office or the purchaser's.

Self-paced training package refers to the kind of package mentioned earlier. The package contains workbook, reference guide, manual, and audio cassettes that operators can use at their own pace to learn a system.

National hotline refers to the availability a toll-free number that operators can call from anywhere in the country to get help.

User groups refers to the existence of groups for people who use a vendor's equipment. These groups encourage users to share ideas and techniques, thus enabling all users to get more from their equipment.

User or vendor newsletter refers to the existence of a newsletter that goes to all purchasers of a vendor's equipment. Like user groups, newsletters also communicate new ideas and techniques, helping users to get more from their equipment.

User reference materials refers to organized, indexed reference material that the trained operator can refer to when he or she has questions. Some of the reference material will duplicate information in training manuals, but not having the training material mixed up with the instructions helps operators to find answers more rapidly.

Built-in system aids take many forms. *On-screen menus* are exhaustive lists of choices an operator can make simply by, say, moving the cursor to the space just before a choice and then touching either the RETURN key or the EXECUTE key. Extensive menus help new operators to learn more rapidly. A HELP command gives operators a quick description of choices they can make. For instance, suppose an operator has forgotten how to print a document. If a HELP feature is available, it will tell him or her enough to get the operation started.

On-screen prompts lead operators through a task step by step. For example, to change all instances of "auto" to "automobile", an operator would touch the REPLACE key. In a line at the top of the screen the system might respond, "Replace what?" He or she would type " auto " and the system would respond "Replace with what?", after which the operator would type " automobile ". Then the system would make the change. During such waits, many systems print a message such as REPLACING, CHECKING, EXECUTING or some such word that lets the operator know that the work is being done (and, therefore, not to continue work until the message disappears). By the way, the spaces before and after " auto " are needed to tell the processor to ignore words such as " automatically ", of which " auto " is only a part. The spaces before and after " automobile " are needed because the characters changed, " auto ", included the spaces before and after " auto " in the sentence.

Turn off or bypass menus/prompts refers to the ability to turn off these helpful features, which take time to list on a work station and time to work through one step at a time. Experienced operators know the steps by heart and can do their work more rapidly when they can turn off the help and execute all steps with a single command or two.

VENDOR SUPPORT AND SERVICE

Vendor support involves (1) the technical assistance needed to make the product work and to maintain and improve the product. Also involved are (2) service of the hardware and (3) the vendors' salespeople's response to purchasing agents. The following paragraphs list and define two categories of service and support.

Office Systems Consultant Support

Site preparation refers to help in getting an office ready to install word processing and can include services that range from consultation on how to arrange staff and furniture to consultation on how and where to lay cables.

Problem solving refers to help on solving problems that occur in the everyday use of the system. Closely related is *application support,* which is help on designing special applications of a system. Some vendors charge for these services, often by the hour.

Help from *systems analysts* is sometimes needed to program, say, the interface between a word processor and a photocompositor.

Maintenance service refers to the quality of maintenance—how good it is, how rapidly a repairman arrives after a service call has been made, and so forth. Closely related is *availability of maintenance service*—where is the service office located? It is best, of course, to have the service office located in your city.

New product announcements refers to the frequency with which a vendor announces new features and the vendor's record for producing announced features on schedule. In general, we don't recommend buying "futures"—features you need that a vendor is promising for "the next release"—because difficulty with product development can delay the actual release. On the other hand, though, you want a vendor that is continually working to upgrade the product so that your system can benefit from future technological developments. Lack of regular announcements may mean that the firm has no development program.

Stability refers to the probability that a vendor will continue in the word processing business. Many firms have failed after a year or two.

Pricing changes refers to the schedule of price changes, which affect not only purchase cost but the on-going cost of supplies and maintenance.

Sales representative support refers to the cooperation (or lack of it) a salesperson gives you and your purchasing office. *Billing support* refers to cooperation in billing your firm for supplies and services in accordance with the firm's requirements. For instance, we ranked several vendors very low because their invoices never provided critical information, such as the purchase order number, that the purchasing staff needs to keep track of an order.

Supplies refers to the availability of supplies and the ability to substitute supplies not manufactured by the vendor of the system. For instance, one of our purchasing agents has a difficult time buying ribbons made by one vendor. She can acquire substitutes at a cheaper price from another vendor, but the system vendor insists that it will not honor the warranty if an operator uses a substitute.

COST

Dollars and Cents

Questions about cost can't be answered in general terms. As a general rule of thumb (Goldfield, 1980a, p. 138), hardware costs should be offset by labor savings within just 18 to 36 months, and many offices recover the costs sooner. One important consideration is that breakthroughs in microelectronics and other technologies have brought cost reductions of 85% and more, and the costs of automated office equipment are expected to continue to drop, especially when compared to general inflationary trends. However, Goldfield expects costs to level off in the near future.

The financial cost of a product includes hardware, software, training, and user support. Hardware charges include a prorated share of the cost of the processing unit, storage devices, site preparation, and annual maintenance. Software charges include a prorated share of the costs of all software products or licenses plus annual maintenance. Training support includes either the vendor's charge for training or a prorated share of the technical support needed to provide in-house training. User support charges include a prorated share of the technical support and operational costs of the system and of the consultants needed to train and assist users, answer questions, and solve problems. The total cost to a user depends on the complexity of the hardware and software and the ease of learning.

Stultz (1982, pp. 204-210) lists the following categories of expense:

- *Capital expense:* the purchase price of the equipment. The firm loses the interest that the capital would have earned, but the loss is offset by tax credits and depreciation. Leasing permits expenses to be written off in present accounting periods, but the cost over time can be much higher than the cost of purchase.
- *Freight expense:* most often, the cost to ship the equipment from the manufacturer's location to the buyer's. Some vendors don't charge freight (which means they have buried this expense in the cost of the system). Some vendors will negotiate this item, others won't. Some buyers will have to hire moving crews to transfer the equipment from the shipping dock to the office.
- *Facilities expense:* sometimes considered a capital cost if classified as a building improvement. Includes installation of electrical power (frequently a computer grade or "isolated power" source to prevent power fluctuations, which damage data), lighting, plumbing (for the development equipment used with a photocomposer), construction of walls or partitions, installation of carpets, and routing of cables.
- *Installation expense:* sometimes done at no additional cost. Some vendors charge either a flat rate or a percentage of the system's purchase price.
- *Occupancy cost:* charges for the space occupied by the equipment, often computed by the square foot.
- *Supply expense:* the monthly or annual cost of storage media, printer ribbons, paper, air filters, print wheels or thimbles, and so forth.
- *Peripheral equipment expense:* includes tables, racks, acoustic covers, cables, connectors, and so forth.
- *Training expense:* sometimes free to a specified number of operators at time of installation, but many vendors have a training charge. If in-house training is planned, managers need to calculate the cost of it.
- *System maintenance:* sometimes included in leasing arrangements. Managers who purchase systems must include the cost of maintenance, which may be provided by contract or on a parts-and-labor basis. If in-house maintenance is planned, managers need to calculate the cost of it.

- *Lost time expense:* losses incurred at installation time, including training and learning time. Managers should also consider later time losses caused by broken equipment.

To get comparable cost figures, design a model system and ask for bids on the whole system. The system could be a microcomputer with printer, word processing software, and printer, or a 100-port shared central system. For instance, one of our RFPs asked vendors to bid on a shared central system that would support 100 work stations and 60 printers.

Cost Savings versus Value-Added Services

A reasonable investment is determined by the applications needed, the equipment proposed, and the range of vendor's prices. One major reason for office automation is to improve productivity. Traditionally, productivity has been viewed as reducing the costs of an operation by trading a costly production method for a less expensive one, and displacing or avoiding costs has been the main cost/benefit justification for office automation: A capital cost replaces a labor cost to increase the operation's efficiency and reduce the need for personnel.

Today, managers must also consider the "value-added" dimension, which focuses on helping individuals and groups of managers and professionals to use their time more effectively. Information technologies enable professionals to create more work. Study findings show that professionals who use dictation and word processing tools provide time savings of $10,000 per professional per year (Marcus, 1981, p. 10).

In a fully automated office, a professional's individual efforts are augmented by the capacity to access, store, structure, and process information. Group problem solving is improved through teleconferencing and file sharing. In fact, office automation has created new means of interfacing, new organizational structures, and new work patterns. The value-added dimensions are difficult to quantify, but they are valid justifications for the use of office automation.

5 How to Assess The Social and Technical Needs of an Organization

The goal of this chapter is to help you assess the social and technical needs of your organization. What is your overall objective for office automation? What are your priorities? What short- and long-run policies and plans would best suit your organization? What is your time line? What are the characteristics of your employees? Chapter 6 follows up with a method for getting a high-quality technical solution to the needs. Chapter 7 shows how to get a high-quality sociotechnical solution to the needs of specific units in your organization.

FORMING A PLANNING TASK FORCE

As the first conversation in Chapter 1 implies, assessment of organizational needs should be done by more than one person. At minimum, a self-employed business person should do the assessment with the help of a secretary. Larger organizations will need to involve many more people at various stages. Useful people to include are an office manager, an experienced administrative secretary, the supervisor of a typing or word processing pool, an

56

experienced user of word processing, a manager of computing operations, a manager of telecommunications, a publications manager, an executive who knows computing, a purchasing agent, a maintenance supervisor, and a plant supervisor who knows the layout of buildings, air conditioning and heating ducts, and so forth. The inclusion of many perspectives helps to ensure objectivity.

MODELING

Stultz (1982, p. 164) recommends preparing models to help you as follows:

- Evaluate what is happening relative to what should be happening.
- Provide a basis for performance goals.
- Identify areas for improvement.
- Provide a basis for cost reduction.
- Detect major errors in business forecasting.
- Test basic cost assumptions.

Models list performance standards, preferably with measurement indexes included. Develop your models with the help of the people who will be responsible for making them happen. When the models have been completed, communicate them to everyone who will be involved in meeting the standards they set. When people at all levels help to make models, they understand how to make them work, and achievement becomes a matter of pride.

One common approach to planning—trending—uses historical data to predict future business objectives. In Stultz's terms (1982, pp. 164-165), trending states what the business *has been doing*. Modeling, in contrast, states what the business *should be doing*.

Stultz recommends "zero-base budgeting," which challenges every element of the business to determine the lowest possible cost, fastest possible cycle time, highest possible quality, and other measurable standards. This approach eliminates useless activities and expenses and avoids doing things just because they've "always been done" or "always been done that way."

Once a model exists, of course, it acts as a base against which to measure performance and evaluate effectiveness. It also helps managers to plan work and to estimate the cost of individual projects. Chapter 7 describes the kinds of cost data to gather for use in a model.

GATHERING GENERAL DATA

Organizational Needs

Basic Considerations.   When you gather general data on organizational needs, concentrate on the whole system and its purposes, not just on steps and processes. You may sometimes find that you can save money without spending a cent on new equipment. One consultant tells of an office that wanted word processing because its personnel frequently used several form letters. On the surface, word processing seemed a natural solution. Then the consultant found out who was receiving those letters—ex-convicts who had been released on probation and whose parole officers were keeping in touch with them! Word processing would have done the job, but there was no gain to be made from using individually typed letters. As a result, the consultant recommended printing form letters with spaces left for the address, salutation, and variable data, which could be typed in before a letter was sent. Using preprinted form letters would be faster and much cheaper than using a word processor.

Study all levels of the organization. Clerical operations are an obvious target for study. In the United States, clerical support staff account for $135 billion annually in wages and fringe benefits, $30 billion in internal support costs, and $50 billion in information resources. In contrast, managers in the United States receive $240 billion annually in wages and fringe benefits and $78 billion in internal support, but only $12 billion in information resources. Similarly, professionals receive $225 billion in wages and fringes and $21 billion for internal support, but only $9 billion for information resources (Goldfield, 1980a, p. 130). Clearly, only the clerical staff receives much support for information resources, yet they account for the smallest amount of wages and benefits.

Not surprisingly, individuals in these three groups have strikingly different perceptions of their productivity. According to a study by Steelcase, Inc. (reported in Goldfield, 1980a, p. 130), most clerical staff members believe they are achieving maximum productivity. In contrast, between 35% and 44% of those in the other categories felt that they weren't doing as much as they felt they could. When asked whether they felt they could do more if conditions were different, between 67% and 77% said yes.

When asked to suggest ways to improve productivity, managers and professionals pointed to reorganization so that work flowed more smoothly from department to department. Most also suggested additional computer terminals, electronic filing, typing, and copying, and telecommunications.

Alex Zellar arrived as his desk at 8:00 A.M., fresh from a trip to meetings in Milwaukee that had cost him most of three work days and had yielded no visible results. He had been certain the study would be approved, but at the last minute the board members had had second thoughts. "Why couldn't they have asked those questions over the 'phone and saved me the trip," Zellar wondered bitterly as he surveyed the litter of memos, letters, reports, and telephone messages that were nesting on his desk. Deep down, he knew the answer: many people don't come to grips with ideas until they arrive at the moment of decision.

Zellar spend much of the morning dictating letters and memos to his secretary. Starting through his in-basket, he found that the tables for the Midwest Division report still hadn't arrived from the computing center. The budget figures had arrived, though, and that meant he could schedule a staff meeting. Buzzing his secretary, he wondered how long it would take to find a time when everyone was free. He earnestly hoped they could meet before Friday.

Don Ragle entered his San Francisco office at 8 A.M., turned on his desktop terminal to organize some data, and then called the New York office. "Are you folks ready?" Receiving an affirmative answer, Don switched on the teleconferencing equipment and started his presentation. As he brought up displays on his terminal, they appeared simultaneously on a terminal in the New York conference room. Occasionally someone would print a copy to examine more closely. Every so often someone would ask a question. Don felt as if he were in New York with them—he could see each participant and knew that they could see him.

One question required more data, which Don accessed quickly and presented. The questioner suggested that Don change his model to use the new data. Don did so. Everyone agreed that the change was an improvement, so Don instructed the computer to replace the original model with the new one. At the end of the presentation the board members voted to accept Don's plans and instructed him to seek bids for the work involved. Don signed off the teleconferencing equipment and sent an electronic memo to Purchasing. The entire meeting took less than an hour.

As Don started through the messages in his electronic in-basket, he reflected on the change electronics had made in his management style. He used to dread trips. They were physically tiring; jet lag bothered him, and he never slept well in a strange bed. Sometimes he needed additional data, as he had today, but couldn't get it on the spur of the moment. Sometimes the travel took up most of two days. Meanwhile, the work back home piled up on his desk. And, of course, sometimes meetings didn't produce any results.

Now he traveled much less even though he participated in more meetings. He rarely had to cope with jet lag and strange beds. He stayed on top of his work at home. And to his surprise, meetings seemed to be more productive, probably because the availability of data and instant reanalysis made it unnecessary to postpone decisions. Post-trip letters and memos no longer took most of a day because he typed them directly into the messaging system.

Don answered the messages in his basket, returned three telephone calls, switched to data processing to complete an analysis, used word processing to finish up a report, and then called up the scheduling module to set up a staff meeting—a process that usually took less than five minutes.

As the vignettes illustrate, the proper equipment saves time and improves management style, yet the statistics quoted earlier show that few managers have installed it. Goldfield found several reasons why executives haven't invested more heavily in office automation: (1) lack of experience and confidence, (2) lack of concrete cost/benefit data, and (3) fear that the equipment might cause more problems than it solves. The fear is caused by the bad press earned by some early installations in which work and social patterns were scrapped without thought for the human cost. The result was stagnation in productivity (sometimes even productivity loss), high job turnover, and disaffection among the leaders who were to direct operations.

Methods. Among the ways to gather data are (1) to analyze needs in a representative cross-section of offices across the organization, (2) to analyze needs throughout a single unit that is typical of the whole organization, (3) to send a questionnaire to every office manager in the organization, (4) as a group, to have the task force list all needs its members are aware of, and (5) to use some combination of these methods.

You may want to use an abbreviated form of the questionnaires at the end of Chapter 7. If you do, keep the form simple and easy to fill out. Remember that its main purpose is to keep you from forgetting anything. Take special care to explain to the staff that the purpose is only to gather data on work processes. You don't want them thinking that next year's raise hinges on the facts and figures you or they record on the questionnaire.

When the task force is satisfied with the list of needs, distribute copies throughout the organization for checking.

Staff Characteristics

Staff characteristics place important limits on managers. As you and other task force members collect data on organizational needs, observe the staff. Is your clerical staff highly skilled or average? Highly motivated? Is staff turnover high or low? How about your executives? How much do they know about modern office technology? Are they generally willing to try something new? Alternatively, is there one division that might be willing to act as guinea pig for a test installation?

For instance, in a university setting many secretaries are

spouses of students, highly intelligent and well educated. For the most part, new technology doesn't threaten them, and many may already have been using text processors on the university's computers. Turnover may be fairly high. Many of the middle managers may have had some experience with computers and may be anxious to try out modern office technology. In contrast, most top administrators will have had little experience with computers, and many will distrust modern technology.

ANALYZING DATA

Number and Kinds of Function

Focus on functions (e.g., originating documents, reviewing documents, sending messages), not on organizational entities (e.g., purchasing, legal department, printing services). Look for substeps within functions. Then challenge the steps and substeps. Stultz (1982, p. 173) suggests several questions:

- What is being done?
- Why is it done?
- Where is it done?
- When is it done?
- Who does it?
- Why do they do it?
- Can it be done somewhere else?
- Can it be eliminated?

Next, match logical flow with functional flow. Look for processes that can be combined, identical equipment that isn't being used to capacity, staff members who are duplicating each other's work, and so forth. Simple reorganization may help you to save space and reduce equipment cost and staff size.

Statement of Needs

The next step, a statement of needs, should identify groups with different needs and list their needs fairly specifically. For instance, most academic settings will have two different general categories of user: (1) administrative users are the professional and staff personnel in offices such as those of the president, vice presidents, school deans, student services, business affairs, and the like; (2) academic users include individual faculty, students, and academic departments. Many other organizations will find parallel categories in (1) most office units and (2) research and development units.

You will probably discover a wide variety of needs, which can be summarized in terms of the categories used in Chapter 4: architecture, features and functions, and other technical capabilities. It's usually safe to assume that all users will have the same needs in terms of training, vendor support and service, and cost.

You will find that all potential users need certain common word processing features such as word wrap, centering, stored words and phrases, insert, delete, global search and replace, simultaneous input and printing, automatic decimal centering, spelling dictionaries, automatic page numbering, math packs, automatic headers and footers, and easy reformatting (see list in Table 6.2, Chapter 6).

You will also find that certain offices have special needs. For instance, we discovered that administrative offices, which often used personalized form letters, had an urgent need for MERGE functions to join letter text with names and addresses in mailing lists. Some wanted to merge letters with mailing lists that already existed on the administrative computer. Some administrative offices needed access to other data bases in the administrative computer, and offices that produced printed matter needed a photocomposition link to the printing plant. Some of the offices wanted electronic mail and message switching within and between campuses.

Academic users worked on short documents such as articles, proposals, reports, and class papers, and on longer documents such as books, extended reports and proposals, theses, and dissertations. Because they work on long documents, they needed (1) extensive storage capability on hard disks, which can best be provided by cluster systems and computer-based text processors. Because they often work with tables, footnotes, and Greek and mathematical symbols, they needed (2) column swapping, floating footnotes, super- and subscripts (preferably shown on the screen), and dual-head printers, which accommodate two different printing elements simultaneously. Because they do more revising than drafting, they needed (3) automatic marking of texts that have been altered by the most recent revision. Because they use computerized data and graphics and sometimes want to include the data and graphs in documents without retyping, they needed (4) easy communication with all academic computers—CDC, DEC, and IBM. Because they write outlines and instructions, they needed (5) automatic paragraph and outline numbering. Because they often work on long documents, they needed (6) automatic tables of contents, lists of tables and illustrations, and indexes. Because they often publish their work, they needed (7) photocomposition interfaces. Because they want to communicate with colleagues elsewhere, they needed (8) electronic mail, message switching, and telecommunications. Because their funds are limited, they needed (9) one terminal for both word and data processing.

For managers the important point is this. Your organization probably will not have these specific needs, but almost surely you'll need to go into considerable detail to avoid leaving out important categories of use.

Staff Characteristics

If your secretaries are educated and skilled, as ours were, they'll be able to handle fairly complex systems, and some of them will prove to be innovators. If turnover is high, though, as ours was, your firm will probably have to give high priority to ease of learning. If your managers have had experience with computers, they will probably want their own terminals and will make excellent use of message switching, scheduling, and other administrative aids. Chances are good, too, that you will have little trouble winning management support for office automation.

RANK ORDERING NEEDS

Rank ordering helps the task force to decide what capability ("backbone application," in Goldfield's term) to install first. Will it be word processing (most commonly it is), electronic mail, message switching, data processing? The important point for managers is: What needs exist, and what is the balance among needs? If you have to sacrifice something, what do you value least? Consider both present realities and long-range plans.

In our case, word processing was the clear candidate for top priority. Electronic mail, message switching, and scheduling were high administrative priorities, whereas sophisticated graphics was a high academic priority. Furthermore, within word processing alone, the university needed nearly every feature and function imaginable, and nearly every office unit needed links between word processors, computers, photocompositors, and other elements. We also knew that the current computing network was unlikely to be changed. Because offices wanted to communicate with it, we had to get systems that would work with it.

When we considered the six major criteria for evaluating modern office technology—architectural and technical specifications, word processing features and functions, other capabilities, ease of learning, vendor service and support, and cost—we realized that the existence of the computing network meant we had to rank architectural and technical considerations first. However, WP features and functions were a close second; when combined with adequate storage and communications, the right functions and features could do a great deal to reduce office overhead. Even if we had to pay more initially for the storage and communications, the university would probably make up the difference in a few years.

Not every firm chooses word processing as the backbone applications. For instance, one firm that we visited had installed a shared system in just one department as a test. Management had found that document typing was uncomplicated and that the greatest need was for executive support systems such as calendar keeping, scheduling, message switching, and electronic mail. It therefore valued word processing features less than features of executive support packages. Eventually that firm chose a highly sophisticated support system and the less sophisticated word processing package that came with the support system.

One interesting sidelight of that firm's study was the discovery of top level executives' concern that the plastic cases of the computer terminals would not suit the décor of executive offices. As a result, one major architectural requirement was terminals in a wood or other suitably appointed case. Eventually that firm chose a brand of terminal that lacked some desirable functional features but suited the décor nicely!

SETTING OBJECTIVES, POLICIES, AND PLANS

Once you have technical needs and staff characteristics in hand, set organizational objectives, policies, and general plans. These should cover questions having to do with technical concurrence, cost justification, shared versus stand-alone systems, general locations, general limits on vendors, and the like. They will govern purchases during the period when you are studying the marketplace, and they will also frame the limits of the organization's eventual decision about hardware and software.

Like us, most large organizations will want to work toward a fully integrated system for word and text processing, but in 1981 such a system did not exist in the marketplace. Furthermore, separate, comprehensive studies by both Indiana University and Stanford University showed that such a system is not likely to become available for several years.

Policies

Most organizations would benefit from adopting two policies on the acquisition and use of word and text processors. One, a *policy of technical concurrence,* requires units to choose software and equipment within a specified range. Our approved list contained a comprehensive line of currently available software options, and regular checks of the marketplace ensure that the approved list continues to contain the best resources available.

The intent was not to be arbitrarily restrictive but rather to make possible a high quality of overall service over the long range.

Our reasons, which would apply equally well to other organizations, are as follows:

1. We wanted to facilitate an interface between pre-existing campus word processors through the computing network.
2. Because IU intended to maintain and repair its own systems, we also wanted efficient and cost-effective maintenance and repair.
3. We wanted to facilitate training and interorganizational job changes by operators.

A second policy, *cost justification,* requires that a purchase request have the support of the requesting unit's administration and of the organization's general administration, and assurance from the requesting unit's management that the software or equipment is cost effective within the unit's budget. Most managers will want this policy to include statements on value-added services as well as on simple cost savings.

A *policy of chargeback,* of interest mainly to other educational institutions and nonprofit organizations, requires that any user of word or text processing will pay the full cost of equipment and operation. Offices that acquire stand-alone word processors and microcomputers will be responsible for the full cost and will maintain them completely from their own resources. Offices that use "ports" into multioffice systems will pay a flat annual rate per port. The charge includes installation and a share of the central word processor. Other peripheral equipment, including terminals, printers, and other nonstandard features, are additional. Users who access text processors on a central computer will pay the same hourly rate for word processing as for data processing.

Short-Range Plans

Because most organizations will want to achieve as much compatibility and integration as is feasible within the available technologies, most managers will want interim guidelines that call for the following:

1. Installing strategically located time-shared, shared-logic, or distributed-logic word processing systems to serve multiple office units. These will be integrated with the computing network.
2. Installing stand-alone word processing systems in units that cannot be served by a shared system. Their software must be compatible with that of the shared systems.
3. Limiting the number and types of word and text processing software and hardware to be installed within the organization.
4. Designating one unit or department as a test site for installation and evaluation. Following the evaluation, managers may either modify plans or proceed with planned installations in other units.

One additional guideline, of interest mainly to academic and research institutions, is:

5. Supporting a limited number of software packages on approved microcomputers for use by individuals and small research project groups.

How to Get
A High-Quality
6 Technical Solution

At this point you have assessed your organization's social and technical needs, ranked in importance the six general criteria for evaluating office automation products, and set policies and general plans. The purpose of this chapter is to help you specify your needs exactly, study the market, and arrive at a high-quality technical answer to the organization's needs.

AN IDEAL SYSTEM

To specify an ideal system, begin with the checklists in Table 4.1. Add any items you need that are not already included. (Definitions of items are in Chapters 3 and 4.) In the far left margin of the checklists mark with an "x" each item that your organization insists on. For instance, if your firm must have communication at a speed of 9600 baud, put an "x" beside that item next to the left margin. Later, when you go out for bids, you will tell vendors not to offer any product that lacks the features marked with an "x".

Next, if you have more than one main category of user, as we did, rank the desirability of each item for each use. For instance, on word processing features and functions, our administrative offices would rarely use scientific equations, but most of our academic offices couldn't get along without them. Thus, we ranked this feature a "1" for administrative uses (neutral) and "3" for academic (highly desirable). Notice that "3" and "x" don't mean the same thing. Items marked "x" must, by definition, also be rated "3", but not all "3s" are necessarily required. For instance, we found "full-page display" highly desirable, but none of our users would be severely handicapped by, say, partial-page display if we had to trade off full-page display for features we needed more. Hence, we marked that feature "3" but not "x".

These codes are not absolute. They represent the value you place on characteristics (1) for your needs and (2) relative to one another without regard to specific products. Later, when you add columns to represent the products you are considering, you'll use another ranking scheme to compare the same feature on different products. In the process, the checklists will become highly useful summary tables for comparing different systems. Tables 6.1 to 6.5 (end of chapter), developed from the checklists, show what completed summaries look like.

Separately, list the amounts of equipment you expect to need and give a physical description of the actual system you hope to acquire. For instance, you might want a single microcomputer with dual diskettes, word processing software, and a letter-quality impact printer with three printing elements. Or, you might need two systems with 60 work stations each, 50 letter-quality printers, 2 twin-track printers, one laser printer, one high-speed draft printer, and a photocomposition interface. One of our models specified 100 work stations and 60 printers.

STUDY DESIGN

The first step in gathering technical data is to design a thorough, systematic study of available resources and to allow enough time to do the study properly. Analysis of the technology will probably take several months. Our organization had a budget of $0.5 billion per year, eight geographic locations, and 10,000 employees. Our formal study took nearly eight months but would have taken at least three months less had we had the tools in this book at the time we started the study.

Before you start gathering data, answer these questions:

- Which vendors will you investigate?
- From what sources will you get data?
- How will you summarize and evaluate the data?

The checklists are your major tool. Your designations of required items and relative desirability are two other important tools. Together, these items give you a set of standards against which to measure the relative performance of different products. Every time you make a decision or design a procedure, write down the details. Keep the descriptions in a notebook or folder. When you prepare your final report, these will describe accurately the method you used to do the study.

CHOICE OF VENDORS

In 1981 more than 100 vendors were offering word processing resources. Unless you have the time to study all of them, you'll need to make an initial assessment of which to cut. For instance, you might eliminate on the basis of characteristics such as presence of sales and service offices in your area, number of years in the word processing field, dollar amount of word processing sales in previous two years, economic stability of firm, offering of shared systems, and so forth.

Alternatively, you could find a subset of vendors and work from that, adding and subtracting vendors on the basis of these same characteristics and any others that occur to you. For instance, we started with 25 firms that were listed in *Information Systems News* (July 28, 1980) as vendors of word processing equipment. Yet, even though this list was supposedly up to date and came from a reputable source, we found it inadequate. For instance, we removed one firm because we could find nothing about its product in *Datapro Reports on Word Processing*. We removed two more because they were not represented in Indianapolis; another because it was going out of business in Indianapolis; and yet another because it had a history of little interest in selling to universities. After adding several more vendors that were recommended by members of the task force, we had a total of 28.

SOURCES OF DATA

There are many sources of data and many ways to combine them. This section lists some of the most helpful and efficient. Our team attended vendor demonstrations (many lasting two hours or more) and sent out a two-part Request for Proposal (RFP) to potential vendors, followed up with telephone calls to clarify responses. Team members telephoned staff members at other institutions (among them Purdue, Ball State, University of Kentucky, University of Wisconsin, Stanford) and visited others (among them Arizona State, Eli Lilly, Proctor & Gamble, Lincoln National Life) to learn what they were doing and to try out systems that we were considering. We tested four systems extensively because representative models had already been installed on one or another of the campuses. Finally, members read widely and attended professional meetings such as CAUSE (an association of university data processing directors) and IWP (International Information/Word Processing Association).

Convention Displays

The IWP sponsors several conventions each year that include seminars by specialists on topics ranging from an introduction to word processing to work flow analysis, training operators, photo-composition, telecommunications, the office of the future, and so forth. By June 1981, when the IWP's Syntopicon IX was held, the number of instructional tracks had expanded to eleven: professional development, planning, implementation and training, industry issues, technology, systems integration, data communications, computer graphics, information management, personnel organization, and special applications. Three days at one of these conventions would give any novice a valuable basic education in modern office technology.

What's more, most vendors display their latest wares at these conventions, giving shoppers a chance to cram a lot of observation into a short period of time. A convention demonstration won't be thorough, but it will let you make a first cut, dropping from consideration products you definitely don't want. Take with you several copies of your checklist. Then do the following:

- Carry your checklists from display to display, asking about the features you would like to require.
- Use a separate checklist for each vendor.
- When a vendor lacks a feature, note that fact and go on to the next question.
- When a vendor has a feature, ask how it works. If possible, get a demonstration so you can see for yourself how easily a feature operates. Rate ease on a scale of 1 to 5, where 1 is extremely hard or awkward and 5 is very easy. (For more details, see the end of this chapter.)
- Sign up to receive literature on vendors' products (for more discussion, see below).

Even in three days, don't expect to be able to survey every vendor unless several of your team are working with you and you've been able to divide up the display hall. With more than 50 vendors displaying and the hours limited to something like 9:00 A.M. to 6:00 P.M., visiting every vendor's display isn't possible, especially if you plan to attend the instructional sessions. Making these cuts at a convention can save you up to half a day per vendor you cut, leaving you more time for demonstrations from vendors that might offer what you need.

A third benefit of attending conventions is the chance to meet and talk with people whose firms have already installed equipment.

Vendors' Literature and Manuals

Ask every vendor whose product you are considering for all their promotional information. Often, if you ask specifically, you can also get users' manuals and training kits to examine. The manuals can be very useful in helping you to decide not only what features and functions a system has but also how usable they are. One important tip: If you have trouble following the instructions in the manuals, so will your staff.

Literature on Word Processing and Office Systems

See Chapter 3 for a listing of reading resources.

Contact with Other Organizations

Contact other organizations like yours. Find out whether they have installed a modern office system, and if so, what. Find out why they chose it, what questions they asked, and how they feel about the choice they made. If they could do it over, what would they do differently? When we first contacted other organizations, inside academe and out, we found an amazing variety of equipment and software, and many combinations within the same firm.

When you have narrowed your list of vendors, ask each for the names of two or three firms near you that use their product. Contact these firms and ask to interview them about the product—why they bought it, what their needs were, how well the product meets their needs, how much equipment failure they've had, how reliable service has been.

Be sure to ask about every item on your lists for ease of learning and vendor support and service. In general, owners aren't biased in the vendor's favor. If an owner says service is good, you can be pretty sure it is. When we asked questions about service and support, we found owners to be helpfully candid.

Private Vendor Demonstrations

Sometimes vendor demonstrations aren't needed. For instance, suppose a research division types many documents that contain complex equations and needs on-screen display of equations. If only one vendor offers that feature, the choice is clear.

Sometimes the choice isn't so clear. Suppose that (1) the

research division needs super and subscripts, floating footnotes (that automatically print on the bottom of the page on which they are referenced), column swapping (for tables), and form letter capability, and (2) three vendors offer all four features. In that case, the task force will want to know ease of use for each feature and each vendor. Similarly, if no vendor offers all the needed features, the task force will want to study ease of use closely and, most likely, reexamine the features it is requiring.

Take a second look at your word processing objectives before seeing a demonstration. Consult your checklists. Give the vendor, in advance, samples of typical work and ask to have them demonstrated. Notice the vendor's response to the request; some word processing systems are too inflexible to accommodate spontaneous changes! Ask for an experienced operator. Also ask to do some actual keyboarding on the basis of other work samples. Schedule the demonstration early in the morning or right after lunch so as to have maximum time. Don't let yourself be scheduled into "quickie" demos preceded or followed by a long lunch.

Apart from helping to prepare for the demonstration, the work samples and an RFP (discussed later) may give small firms a boost by telling the vendor that the organization is serious about a purchase. Most vendors favor large organizations over small ones because the potential sale is larger. As a result, small firms sometimes have trouble getting a vendor of commercial word processors to take them seriously. (Vendors of microcomputers with word processing software aren't quite so neglectful.)

Be wary if a vendor tries to talk you into a demonstration at the site of a firm that has purchased its product. It may mean that the vendor has a small, unstable sales and service base in your area.

However, if you do decide to attend a demonstration at a purchaser's site, look for opportunities for private conversation with the word processing supervisor, users, and anyone else actively involved with the system. Ask (confidentially, of course) about breakdowns, speed of service, ease of use, and any topic about which the demonstration left questions in your mind. You might also ask why the firm is willing to take time from its work to do demonstrations! If the vendor's salespeople stick to your team members like glue, making private conversation impossible, simply set up a luncheon appointment at the earliest possible time.

Before a demonstration list the questions you want answered and the features you want demonstrated. Give copies of the list to others who will see the demonstration. It helps to have:

- More than one person trying to get information.
- One person responsible for checking off items on checklists.
- Another person responsible for writing or tape recording answers to questions.

When possible, take the entire task force to demonstrations. In addition, take one or two people who will actually use the equipment (if the task force does not already contain such people). Tell everyone to observe the vendor's operation and the professionalism of the demonstrating staff. Be prepared to push hard for answers to questions. Don't be surprised to encounter defensiveness. We met it with several (although not all) vendors. The market is highly competitive, and the vendors are anxious to make a sale, especially to a large organization. They don't want to give information that will help you to compare directly their product with that of other vendors. They would much prefer to impress you with the unique features of their product.

Sharon Tiffany (1979) counsels shoppers to seek information on the following:

- *Ease of operation and required training time.* You need to know whether the equipment requires a highly technical operator.

- *Costs.* You need to know the total costs of hardware, software, and media. Also check for hidden costs such as fees for installation, training, maintenance, delivery, and adding onto the equipment in the future.

- *Flexibility of equipment.* Can you tailor the hardware set-up to your proposed workflow? Can you add to it or upgrade it to greater capability as your needs grow? If so, what are the costs?

- *Service.* How many qualified service technicians are in your area? And how soon after you call will they arrive?

- *Customer support.* Most vendors offer a training instructor who is an expert on the equipment and will be available to you, as needed, to assist with ongoing questions and problems. If you are purchasing a word processor for the first time, you may need help in writing procedures, hiring personnel, educating users and operators on what to expect and how to use the new service, measuring productivity, setting up workflow, and creating logging and filing systems. You'll want to know whether the vendor has a qualified individual to help you in these areas.

When you leave a demonstration, take with you literature that describes the equipment and financial reports on the vendor. When you have finished all vendor demonstrations, complete the criteria tables and summarize your notes.

Demonstration Projects

The task force may wish to visit a demonstration project such as Micronet Inc.'s The Paperless Office in the Watergate Mall Complex in Washington, D.C. Micronet, a management consulting firm, spend nine months developing a system that would integrate commercially available products. Larry Stockett, the company's chief executive officer, worked through the technical problems posed by incompatible equipment and talked 14 vendors into leasing him hardware and computer programs at nominal cost. Today the Paperless Office uses $2 million of automated office equipment from 22 manufacturers. Nearly 8000 people, including top managers from many large firms, have visited the site to see how the office of the future works.

All staff members work from terminals on their desks and take portable terminals with them on trips. The Office staffers haven't actually eliminated paper, but they use much less of it. In staff member Bonnie Canning's words. "We believe that no one medium—paper, electronic, micrographic—is perfect. We use each for its strengths and avoid its weaknesses [Brairton, 1981, p. 43]."

Vendor Analysis of Needs

Some vendors, taking advantage of managerial confusion about office automation, offer to do a free analysis of needs. We agree with Penn (1981), who recommends strongly that managers stay away from such offers. Penn has never seen any such study that (1) did not recommend automated equipment or (2) recommended another vendor's product.

Request for Proposal (RFP)

A Request for Proposal (RFP) for word processing products, a tool to get comparable bids for the same product, should contain (1) a detailed checklist of ranked criteria such as those in Table 4.1, (2) definitions of the criteria, and (3) a detailed list of input and output hardware and software. When you put together the checklist and the list of equipment, you'll have the basis for an RFP that you can send to all potential vendors and expect to receive price quotations that are comparable even though the architecture of the systems may differ considerably.

The reason for this amount of detail is the lack of standardization. If you ask only for the price of a "shared system" and then ask what it includes, you'll find that at least one system serves up to 60 terminals, another serves up to 24, and another serves only 16. If you continue to inquire, you might learn that on the third system, half of the 16 must be stand-alone work stations. (Not surprisingly, then, the cost per work station for the third system is more than that for the first, whose work stations are ordinary intelligent terminals linked to a minicomputer-based software package.)

To assure yourself of comparable bids, be sure to specify the following:

- Number of work stations, printers, and so forth
- Special features (e.g., horizontal scroll, math packages)
- Type fonts, or styles
- Size and speed of printers (e.g., wide carriage, draft, twin track)
- Cabling required
- Delivery schedule
- Amount of storage (e.g., disk size, number of diskettes)
- Communication requirements
- Backup capabilities
- Security

You might be surprised at the relative lack of response to the RFP. Our original RFPs were sent out in August 1980. Because some vendors were slow in responding, we sent follow-up letters in October 1980. Follow-up telephone calls were made in November, December, and January to solicit additional or missing information. Members of our task force met with vendors' representatives to discuss the process and the products.

Of the 28 vendors to whom we sent RFPs, only 20 submitted bids. We divided the responses into two lists. One contained all vendors of stand-alone systems; the other, all vendors of multi-terminal systems. Only eight responded with proposals for true shared systems. Some vendors appeared on both lists.

We found that we couldn't compare costs on the multiterminal systems because they accommodated varying numbers of printers, terminals, and other peripherals. To get comparable prices, we developed a model system for administrative users and another for academic users and sent out new RFPs to the vendors who offered these systems. Cost rankings of shared systems were made on the basis of responses to this RFP.

Leasing and Testing

Still another source of data is a lease-purchase arrangement. Perhaps you are pretty certain one type of equipment is what you want, but you have some questions. For instance, you might need communications to an XYZ computer, and the vendor is promising it for a date six months or so into the future. You don't want to be saddled with the equipment if the vendor doesn't deliver as promised. So, you arrange for lease or lease-purchase until the specified date arrives. If the vendor doesn't deliver, you terminate the lease and get other equipment.

Perhaps you simply want to try out several kinds of equipment for a period of time before making a choice. Leasing can make that possible. We would issue a warning, though. Two of our consistent findings were:

- No matter how bad a product proved to be in comparison to other products, the users fell in love with it because it was so much better than a typewriter. A few users even fell in love with an unusually difficult time-shared text processor!
- Once people get documents stored on a processor, they don't want to switch. They've learned how to run the machine, and they don't want to rekeyboard.

Optical character reading (OCR) technology can solve the rekeyboarding problem, but it won't change people's feelings. Before our shared systems were installed, a few offices had acquired stand-alone equipment that was not compatible with our computer network or with our word processors. Later, in most cases, we had difficulty persuading people to change. So, our advice is to avoid leasing several brands, even for test purposes. You'll only buy personnel problems along with the opportunity to test.

ANALYSIS AND SUMMARY

Rating Scales

To summarize and systematize the data, use tables like those in Tables 6.1 to 6.6, which are simple expansions of the checklists in Chapter 4. Code the entries to reflect your earlier judgments about required characteristics (the "x" mark next to the left margin) and relative desirability of characteristics for specific uses (in the sample tables, our judgments about desirability are in the columns marked "Adm" and "Ac.".

Next, rate each product in terms of the items on the checklists. For each item we used a scale of 0 (zero) to 5, where: 0 = does not exist in the product, and 5 = excellent feature, very easy or convenient to use. This scale helped us to compare the same feature across products. The judgments are somewhat subjective, and the ability to judge improves with experience. If time permits, when data gathering is nearly complete, task force members may want to review their judgments on the first two or three products rated.

Checklist in hand, Susan Jacobs walked up to Vendor A's demonstration and asked to see how underlining was done. The demonstrator touched the AUTO key, followed by the underline key. Then he began typing a heading. The underline appeared on the screen when the character appeared. At the end of the heading, he touched AUTO again to stop underlining. "What happens it I want to underline something I typed earlier?" Jacobs asked.

"You move the cursor to the beginning of the first word you want to underline. Then you type the underline key once for each character

you want to underline. After the last letter you want to underline, touch the execute key and you'll be able to type just characters." Watching, Jacobs could see the underlining snaking across the screen.

That technique was much easier than Vendor B's—that product had no automatic key, and the demonstrator had had to touch the underline key after each character that was to be underlined. Vendor C's product hadn't been much better. All Vendor C offered was a process like the second one Vendor A had demonstrated.

"Can I get either solid or character-by- character underlining?" she asked.

"No, but that's coming in the next release."

Moving on to the demonstration of a software package on a microcomputer, Vendor D, Jacobs again asked to have underlining demonstrated. This time the demonstrator touched the CONTROL key and then "O" and "S" in rapid succession. Then he typed the words to be underlined. Then he repeated the "CONTROL-O-S" sequence. On the screen Jacobs could see "$\wedge$SHeading$\wedge$S." The printed underline would appear only in the hard, or printed, copy. She found it hard to imagine the underlining, and she wondered how she would remember the key sequence that started and stopped the underlining. Furthermore, she discovered, underlining would always be character by character. The package didn't include solid underline.

Stopping at the demonstration of Vendor E, who offered a "programmable" package, she repeated her request. This time the demonstrator typed the shift key and the underline key at the same time, putting a single underline mark on the screen. Then he typed the heading, followed by another "shift-underline" to "turn off" the underlining. The "shift-underline" connection wasn't hard to remember, but Jacobs still found it hard to imagine what the printed result would look like. One good feature, though, was that she could get either solid or character-by-character underlining just by typing either "UNS" or "UNC" in a list of commands at the beginning of the file.

Sitting down with her ranking sheet, she decided that Vendor A won the competition hands down. The AUTO key was easy to use and would save many keystrokes. She gave that product a "5." Vendor B's product was a real time waster—double keystroking was for typewriters, not word processors. It deserved a "1". Vendor D's "CONTROL-O-S" was awkward but used fewer keystrokes than Vendor B's product, so she ranked it "2." She liked the products of Vendors C and E better than D's product, but not as well as A's. Vendor C's product offered no automatic key, but the underlining showed on the screen. Vendor E's product would use fewer keystrokes, but the underlining didn't show. She decided that neither deserved a "2," so she ranked both "3."

Tucking her clipboard under her arm, she started back down the aisles. Now she had a solid idea how to evaluate underlining on other products.

Jacobs' partner, Virginia Wells, was evaluating pagination. Vendor A's product had a PAGE key. After finishing a revision, operators moved the cursor to the top of the document and pressed PAGE. The cursor moved to the last line that would print on the first page. If the break was acceptable, the operator said "OK" by pressing the EXECUTE key. If it wasn't, the operator used one of the cursor moving keys (marked with arrows that point up, down, left, or right) to move the cursor up or down, and then pressed EXECUTE. The process was easy to follow, but Virginia thought it would be time-consuming on a long document. "Is there a way I can get it to do the paging automatically? On rough drafts our operators won't care where a page ends."

"No," replied the demonstrator.

"Could I give the system certain rules, such as no widow lines and no headers at the bottoms of pages, and have it paginate the parts that aren't affected by the rules?"

"No, but that's an interesting idea. I'll pass that one along to our development division."

"Can I force a new page? A title page, for instance, would have only a few lines of typing on it, but I'd want the table of contents to start on a new page."

After receiving an affirmative response, Wells moved on to Vendor B's product, which had no pagination feature because each page was created as a separate file (in other words, "page-oriented," not "document-oriented"). Wells could tell that substantial revision would probably force retyping. Vendor B's product might work for one-page letters but not for documents.

Vendor C's product paginated automatically but didn't show page breaks on the screen. What the operator saw was a stream of text rather like a scroll that rolled up at the top and out at the end. The product allowed operators to force a page, and even allowed "conditional page" statements—if this header or first line of paragraph would normally start on a bottom line, start a new page instead; if the last line of a paragraph will print at the top of a page, back up, grab the next-to-last line, and print the two lines at the top of the new page.

Vendor D's product marked page breaks as the operator typed. If a page break marker appeared and the break wasn't appropriate, the operator could put in a new break manually.

Vendor E's product paginated automatically on screen, but changing the breaks took several steps.

Wells decided that Vendor D's product deserved a "5", Vendor B's, a "0". Vendor E's feature was awkward to use, so she rated it "1". Vendor A's product allowed operators to control pagination but might cost considerable time. Vendor C's product automated the process but didn't show the breaks on the screen. Wells finally decided on a "3" rating for both.

Table 6.1   Sample Ratings of Architectural and Technical Features[a]

Features	Uses		Software					
	Ac.	Adm.	V-1	V-2	V-3	V-4	V-5	V-6
Hardware Devices								
x Flexible Mix Between Printer/CRTs	3	3	24	18	24	18	24	18
x Cable Distance Minimum ____'	3	3	24	24	24	24	24	0
x Foreground/Background Operations	3	3	18	18	18	0	18	24
x Communcation Speed 9600 BAUD	3	3	18	18	18	18	18	0
x RJE 3780 Emulation	3	3	18	18	24	24	0	18
CICS/3270 Protocol	1	3	0	0	4	3	5	2
Optimum Number of Devices								
Academic: 60	3	1	12	9	9	9	9	3
Administrative: 24	1	3	3	3	3	3	3	1
x Async. Comm.	3	1	30	12	0	18	0	18
Subtotal			147	120	124	117	101	84
Printers								
x Queuing	3	3	18	18	18	0	18	12
Twin Track	3	3	9	9	0	0	0	9
Wide Track	3	3	9	9	0	0	0	9
Draft Speed	3	3	12	12	9	9	12	6
Cut Sheet Feeder	3	3	9	9	9	9	9	9
Envelope Feeder	1	2	3	3	0	0	0	0
Subtotal			60	60	36	18	30	45
Document Storage								
x Hard Disk Capability- Minimum 3MB	3	3	18	18	18	18	18	18
x Expandable Disk	3	3	18	18	18	18	18	18
Floppy Disk Capacity	2	2	0	8	0	6	2	6
Subtotal			36	44	36	42	38	42

Features	Uses		Software					
	Ac.	Adm.	V-1	V-2	V-3	V-4	V-5	V-6
Terminals								
Full-Page Display	2	2	0	0	0	0	0	0
Partial-Page Display	3	3	9	9	9	9	6	9
Local Intelligence	3	3	0	9	0	15	0	6
Detachable Keyboard	3	3	9	0	9	9	9	0
Tilt Screen	2	2	0	0	0	0	0	0
Magnification	1	1	9	0	0	0	0	0
Subtotal			27	18	18	33	15	15
TOTALS			270	242	214	210	184	186
Ranking			*1*	*2*	*3*	*4*	*6*	*5*

[a] These data are fictitious.
[b] *Use Key:* Each characteristic was assigned a desirability value for academic or administrative uses. *Software Rating Key:* Product performance characteristics were rated on a scale from 0 to 5, where 0 = not available and 5 = excellent. These ratings were multiplied by the desirability value. Next, scores on required items were doubled. Overall, vendors are ranked from 1 to 6 for highest to lowest total score.

Use Rating Scale:

x = Required Item
3 = Highly Desirable
2 = Desirable
1 = Neither Desirable nor Undesirable

Software Rating Scale:

5 = excellent
4 = above average
3 = average
2 = below average
1 = poor
0 = nonexistent

Table 6.2 Sample Ratings of WP Features and Functions[a]

Feature/Function	Uses		Software					
	Ac.	Adm.	V-1	V-2	V-3	V-4	V-5	V-6
Display								
Scrolling	3	3	6	9	9	9	3	12
Horizontal								
Vertical								
Exact Image of Print	3	3	0	0	0	0	0	0
Sub- and Superscripts	3	2	0	0	0	0	0	8
Control Code Display	2	3	6	6	6	6	6	6
Greek and Math	3	2	0	0	0	0	0	7
Multicolumn	2	2	6	6	6	6	0	6
Associated								
Snaked								
Subtotal			18	21	21	21	9	39

Table 6.2 Sample Ratings of WP Features and Functions[a] (Continued)

Feature/Function	Uses		Software					
	Ac.	Adm.	V-1	V-2	V-3	V-4	V-5	V-6
Automatic Features								
x Word Wrap	3	3	18	18	18	18	18	18
x Margin Adjust	3	3	18	18	6	18	18	24
x Decimal Tab	3	3	18	18	18	18	12	18
Input Underline	3	3	9	9	0	0	6	9
x Centering	3	3	18	18	18	18	12	24
Boldface	2	2	6	6	2	6	4	8
x Line Spacing	3	3	18	24	18	18	12	18
x Page Numbering	3	3	18	18	18	18	18	18
x Header/Footer	3	3	18	18	18	18	18	24
x Pagination	3	3	18	18	18	18	12	24
x Repagination	3	3	18	18	18	18	12	18
Widow Line Adjust	3	3	9	6	0	0	9	9
x Footnote Control	3	2	12	12	24	18	18	18
Subtotal			198	201	176	186	169	230
Miscellaneous								
x Stored Words/Phrases								
x Mailing List/Merge	3	3	24	18	18	18	18	18
Multicolumn	2	2	6	6	6	0	6	10
Forms Fill-in	2	3	6	8	6	4	2	8
Revision Marking	3	3	9	9	6	0	9	9
x System Security	3	3	18	18	18	18	18	18
Scientific Equations	3	2	0	9	0	0	0	8
x Records Management	3	3	24	30	0	12	24	18
Tbl of Contents Gen.	3	3	9	9	0	9	9	0
Index Generation								
x Temporary Margin	3	3	18	18	6	18	18	24
Hyphenation help	3	3	9	9	0	0	9	12
x Doc. Assem/Merge	3	3	18	24	18	0	18	18
x Search	3	3	18	18	18	18	6	18
x Sel Search/Replace	3	3	18	18	18	18	6	18
x Block Move/Copy	3	3	18	18	18	18	6	24
x Column Move/Delete	3	3	18	18	18	0	0	18
x Sort, Alphanumeric	3	3	24	24	18	18	18	18
Spelling Dictionary	2	2	8	0	0	6	6	0
Proportional Space	3	3	9	0	0	0	9	9
Justification	3	3	9	9	9	0	9	9
Global Search/Replace	3	3	9	9	9	9	9	9
Index Generation	3	3	9	9	0	9	9	9
Subtotal			281	281	186	175	209	275
TOTALS			497	503	383	382	387	547
Ranking			*3*	*2*	*4*	*6*	*5*	*1*

[a] See footnote for Table 6.1 for keys to table.

Table 6.3 Sample Ratings of Other Capabilities

Features	Uses		Software					
	Ac.	Adm.	V-1	V-2	V-3	V-4	V-5	V-6
Other Capabilities								
Data Processing	1	3	1	9	12	12	0	0
Math	3	3	9	9	9	3	0	12
Electronic Mail	3	3	0	12	9	9	6	0
Message Switch	3	3	9	12	9	9	6	9
Graphics	3	3	6	0	0	0	0	12
Scheduling	3	3	0	0	9	0	0	0
OCR Input	3	3	9	9	9	9	9	9
Photocomp. Output	3	3	9	12	9	9	9	9
TOTALS			43	63	66	51	30	51
Ranking			*5*	*2*	*1*	*3*	*6*	*3*

KEYS: See footnote for Table 6.1 for keys to use.

Table 6.4 Sample Ratings of Ease of Learning

Category	Software					
	V-1	V-2	V-3	V-4	V-5	V-6
Classes for Trainers	2	3	0	2	3	2
Classes for Users	3	3	3	3	3	3
Self-Paced Trng Pkg. (Customer's site)	3	5	3	2	1	2
National Hotline (800)	3	3	0	3	0	3
User Groups	4	4	2	0	0	2
User or Vendor Nwsltr	4	4	3	3	3	3
User Ref. Materials	4	4	3	3	1	3
Built-in System Aids						
On-screen menus	3	3	1	2	0	0
Help command	3	0	3	3	0	0
On-screen prompts	3	3	2	2	1	3
Turn off/bypass menus/prompts	3	3	1	3	0	2
TOTALS	35	35	21	26	12	23
Ranking	*1*	*1*	*5*	*3*	*6*	*4*

Table 6.5 Sample Ratings of Vendor Support and Service

Category	Software					
	V-1	V-2	V-3	V-4	V-5	V-6
Office Systems Consultant Support						
Site preparation	4	4	3	3	4	3
Problem solving	2	2	3	3	1	2
Application support	3	3	3	3	3	3
Systems analysts	3	3	3	3	3	2
Maintenance service	2	2	2	2	3	2
Avail. of maint serv	2	3	2	2	3	2
New proc. announce.	3	4	3	3	3	4
Subtotals	19	21	19	19	20	18
Purchasing Support						
Pricing changes	2	2	2	2	4	3
Sales rep. response	2	1	2	1	4	4
Billing support	1	1	2	2	4	5
Supplies	3	1	2	2	3	3
Subtotals	8	5	8	6	15	15
TOTALS	27	26	27	26	35	33
Ranking	*3*	*5*	*3*	*5*	*1*	*2*

Table 6.6 Sample Chart of Costs[a]

Vendor	Rank	No. of Proc.	Total $ Hardware	Total $[b] Software	$ Sub Total	4 Years Mainten.	$ Totals
For Academic Uses							
V-1	1	2	$ 738,359	$ 42,450	$ 780,809	$262,176	$1,042,985
V-2	2	5	842,432	—0—	842,432	344,400	1,186,832
V-3	6	1	1,269,500	36,260	1,305,760	441,216	1,746,976
V-4	3	100	1,044,000	2,592	1,046,592	432,000	1,478,592
V-5	4	1	1,014,565	82,814	1,097,379	413,820	1,511,199
V-6	5	7	1,141,678	8,022	1,149,700	400,896	1,550,396
V-7	7	100	1,022,238	134,450	1,156,688	604,800	1,761,088
For Administrative Uses							
V-1	1	2	$ 738,350	$ 33,650	$ 772,000	$262,176	$1,034,176
V-2	2	5	842,432	—0—	842,432	344,400	1,186,832
V-3	3	7	1,021,725	6,650	1,028,375	339,360	1,367,735
V-4	4	100	1,044,000	864	1,044,864	432,000	1,476,864
V-5	5	1	1,014,565	82,814	1,097,379	413,820	1,511,199
V-6	6	7	1,141,678	8,022	1,149,700	400,896	1,550,596
V-7	7	100	1,022,238	78,400	1,100,638	604,400	1,705,038

[a] Vendors bid on a system to include 100 terminals and 60 printers.
[b] Includes purchase price and annual charges for four-year period.

When we computed the scores, we used summary tables. We multiplied scores by desirability value (DV below) and then doubled the scores for required items. For example, take the scores from the foregoing vignettes. The raw scores look like this:

Feature	DV	Vendor A	Vendor B	Vendor C	Vendor D	Vendor E
x Underlining	3	5	1	3	2	3
x Pagination	3	3	0	3	5	1

Multiplied by desirability value, the scores look like this:

Feature	DV	Vendor A	Vendor B	Vendor C	Vendor D	Vendor E
x Underlining	3	15	3	9	6	9
x Pagination	3	9	0	9	15	3

If the features were not required, the doubled scores would remain as is. However, the "x" in the left margin tell us that these features are required. To make products with required features stand out in our summary tables, we doubled the scores for required features. These same scores, doubled, would look like this:

Feature	DV	Vendor A	Vendor B	Vendor C	Vendor D	Vendor E
x Underlining	3	30	6	18	12	18
x Pagination	3	18	0	18	30	6

Finally, we totaled the scores for each vendor and ranked the vendors by total score. For instance, if these were the only features considered, the vendors' total scores and ranks would look like this:

Feature	DV	Vendor A	Vendor B	Vendor C	Vendor D	Vendor E
x Underlining	3	30	6	18	12	18
x Pagination	3	18	0	18	30	6
TOTAL		48	6	36	42	24
Rank		1	5	3	2	4

The Final Choice

As you make your final choice for the organization, observe Tiffany's (1979) cautions on some of the common hazards of equipment selection:

- Don't choose on hardware alone. Consider the total package—hardware, software, people, service, and support.
- Don't choose a product just because you like the vendor. After purchase you'll be dealing mostly with service and support personnel, so get to know those people, too.

- Don't buy "futures." [We made that mistake on one item. It had been promised for January 1981 but was not delivered until April 1981.]
- Don't let deadlines control your choice. You'll be happier in the long run if you wait a bit for the right equipment than if you buy something inferior simply because you can get it next week.
- Don't decide solely on what's needed now. Consider your office's future and the vendor's future plans. How well do they mesh?
- Don't forget to bargain for extras. For instance, if you have documents already prepared that your staff will have to keyboard into the new processor, bargain with the vendor to enter the documents for you via optical scanner and give you diskettes with the documents on them. Also bargain for discounts for quantity. The larger the order, the greater the bargaining power.

A word processor is a large investment, even when rented or leased. It ties up a substantial amount of money in storage media, supplies, personnel training, and so on. Make sure the equipment won't quickly become obsolete and cost more to replace than you would have had to pay for the right equipment in the first place.

7

Office Units:
Planning
And Implementation

To this point, many of you won't have spent a nickel on any product except, possibly, for testing purposes. Your main purpose has been simply to identify the products that would best serve and be most cost-effective for your organization *should any unit decide to install automated office equipment.* Now you are ready to plan or to supervise planning of the first installation. If yours is a small firm, you may already have picked the products you want to install. Your goal now is to accomplish effective installation, training, and evaluation.

Remember that a technical solution will yield the benefits expected of it only if an organization's staff accepts it. This chapter tells how to plan for specific offices and departments and discusses the steps necessary for successful installation and later evaluation. The strategy is based on the thesis that staff more readily accept plans in which they "own" part of the development. Because the office is a critical sociotechnical system (Bostrom, 1980), the study method deals with both technical and social factors.

THE SOCIOTECHNICAL FRAMEWORK

As Figure 7.1 shows, each office or department unit is composed of a technical system and a social system. The technical system consists of inputs (words, data, appointments, pictures, etc.) that are processed through specific tasks (origination, production, reproduction, filing, distribution, etc.) using technology (word or data processing, photocomposition, graphics, message switching, etc.) to yield meaningful outputs (documents, tables, graphs, schedules, copies, etc.). The purpose of the technical system is to accomplish tasks. The people who carry out the tasks are organized into job roles and office structures—a social system whose focus is the quality of work life of the unit and its members.

Because the two systems continually interact, the introduction of any modern office technology will change the nature of roles and tasks within and across office units. The changes themselves are neutral—neither good nor bad. For managers the important fact is that staff members *will* perceive the changes as either good or bad and will support or resist them accordingly. For instance,

Dilbert Legal Services had had its office automation equipment in place for six months, now, and Ed Jamison was still amazed by the changes it had brought about. Studies had shown that the largest time consumer in the organization was intrastaff communication and scheduling. Therefore, the firm had acquired a highly sophisticated message-switching, calendar-keeping, and scheduling module. Jamison had expected the time savings that had come from automatic scheduling, and he welcomed it.

The surprise was the change in the messages he received. Before the new system, his secretary had rarely suggested ideas for change in the office. Don Lincoln, who managed several large accounts, rarely communicated except through occasional long memos that were so crammed with jargon as to be nearly unreadable. Jamison had never liked wading through them. Now, when he signed on in the morning, he often found brief memos from both parties. "It struck me that . . .", "What if we were to . . .", "Ed, on the Jones account, we could finish the brief much more quickly if we . . . . What do you think?" Most of the ideas were good, or soon led to good ideas, and action got underway immediately. The whole organization had a freer, more flexible feel. Jamison didn't know why the message switching system made people feel freer, but clearly it did, and he felt the change was for the better.

Dilbert Legal Services had had its office automation equipment in place for six months, now, and Ed Jamison was dubious about the changes it had brought about. Studies had shown that the largest

INPUTS
Words
Data
Dates
Pictures

OUTPUTS
(PRODUCT OR SERVICES)
Documents
Schedules
Graphs

TECHNICAL SYSTEM

SOCIAL SYSTEM

TECHNOLOGY

ROLES/STRUCTURE

TASKS

PEOPLE

ENVIRONMENT

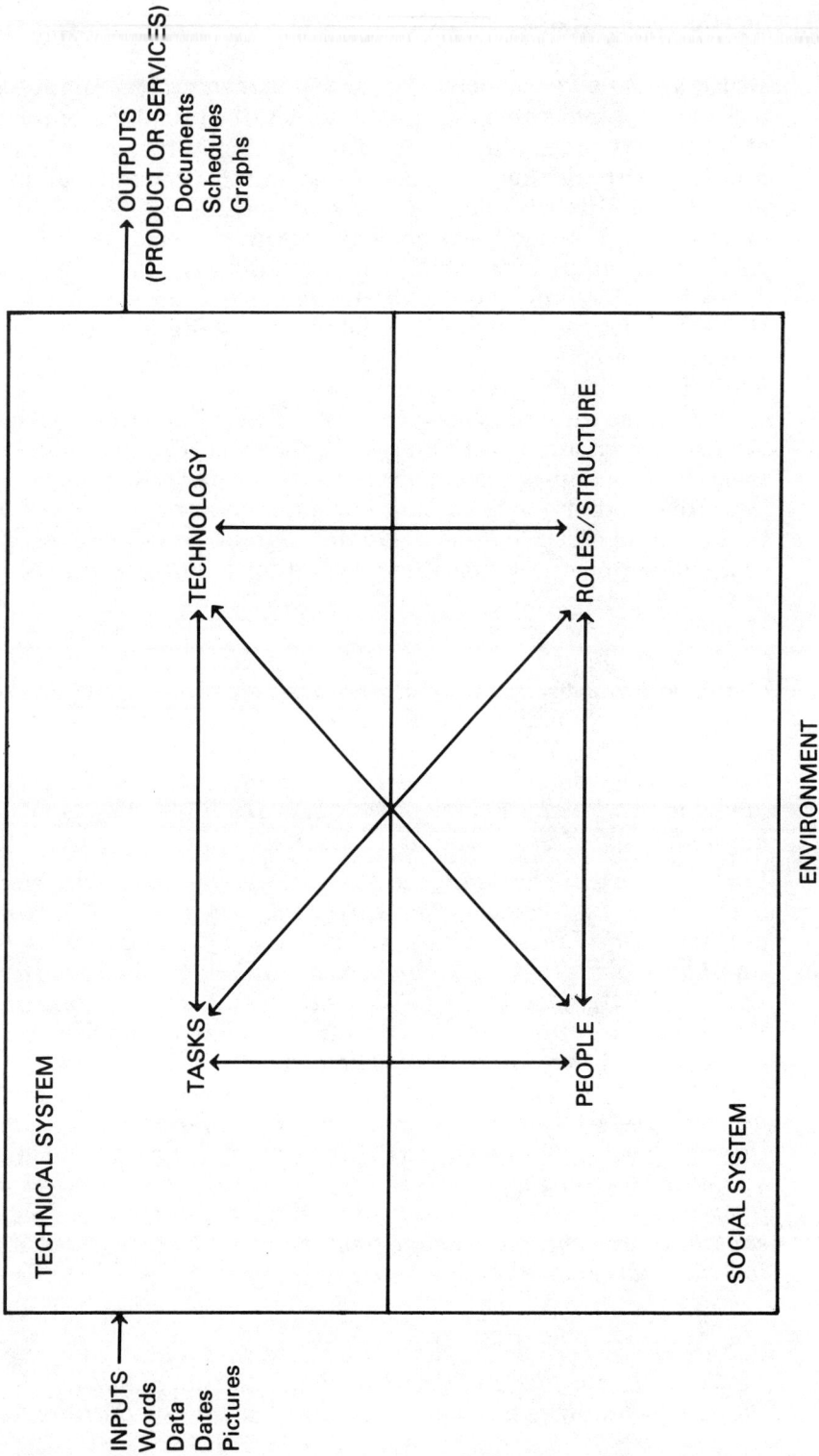

Figure 7.1 An Organizational Work System Viewed as an Open Socio-Technical System

*time consumer in the organization was intrastaff communication
and scheduling. Therefore, the firm had acquired a highly sophisticated message-switching, calendar-keeping, and scheduling module.
Jamison wasn't very happy about having his calendar on the
system—it didn't seem real. And meetings were too easy to schedule.
Every time he signed on, he found requests for meetings. He
wondered when he was ever going to be able to slip away for a round
of golf.*

*The worst thing was the messages. Tons of them, it seemed. His
secretary, who used to be very respectful of his time and his position,
had changed. Now she was full of new ideas, and all of them wound
up in his in-basket. Did she think she was as smart as he was? If
those ideas were any good, he'd have thought of them! And Don
Lincoln, who handled several large accounts—the same thing had
happened to him. No formal typed memos, just short frequent ones
that demanded action now, just by the fact of being there. Jamison
didn't like it. He felt that his personal space had been invaded and
office life would never be the same again.*

The same office, the same events, two different reactions. The
situation isn't fiction. It existed in one of the firms we visited and
probably will in your firm, too. Whether your staff view neutral
happenings as good or bad will depend on how you handle the social
dynamics. One major factor in success will be whether the plans for
office automation have the full support of top management.
Throughout the planning process, then, keep top executives
informed and involved as much as possible.

For individuals, quality of work life depends on how well their
skills and preferences suit the available office roles and tasks. They
want to be able to do satisfactory work and satisfy their personal
needs for recognition, influence, learning opportunities, wages, and
working conditions (Bostrom, 1980).

THE PLANNING PROCESS

Planning and implementing office automation involves (1) determining the need for and acceptance of automation and (2) developing
a detailed implementation plan. For any given office, what are its
greatest operational inefficiencies? What equipment would make
the greatest initial impact? Which staff members appear to feel
enthusiastic about automation? What are the staff members' needs
and personal desires? What is the office manager's attitude?

Determining Needs and Acceptance

Determining needs and acceptance requires managers (1) to
quantify the technical needs of the office unit and (2) to discover the
level of acceptance.

Brief the personnel. The first step toward these goals is to brief all key managers individually on office automation, general organizational directions, and scope of planning to date. The purpose is to communicate decisions, policies, and terminology involved with the project. After the briefing, when possible, ask whether the managers wish to proceed. (In some cases managers may not have a choice; change may be a mandate from the Chief Executive Officer.) The simple fact of the briefing, which imputes a value to the managers' wishes, may elicit initial acceptance.

Next, discuss with each manager whether to have a briefing for his or her whole staff. If a briefing is held, it should be concisely done and should last no more than an hour, including plenty of time for questions. In the meeting define terms, explain the scope of the project, specify what is expected of the individuals in the unit, and introduce the outside agents—office systems consultants—who will help in the endeavor. (For more on consultants, see Chapter 8.)

Choose a project coordinator. Choose a project coordinator from among the staff members in the office to be studied. The coordinator, who will work directly with the consultants, will do a technical study of the needs of his or her individual office unit. This person should be highly visible and well accepted by all staff members. The office consultants will train the coordinators with intensive work on terminology, scope of the project, and use of data-gathering instruments.

Collect data. Everyone begins an assessment with some idea about what needs exist. In a given office, perhaps, ordinary letters sits in the typing stack for two or three days, form letters tie up the staff for days at a time, and reports and proposals take two weeks or longer. The absence of a typist for a day or more causes a major crisis.

On the managerial side, perhaps the manager is almost never in the office because he or she travels so much. Work piles up on the desk. Subordinates' work gradually slows to a halt because the manager isn't there to make the necessary decisions. Although he takes work home at night, he never quite catches up before leaving on the next trip. Scheduling meetings can take half a day or more of the personal secretaries' time.

Data gathering digs out specific facts such as how many ordinary letters the office staff types each week, and how long (on the average) each letter takes. How many kinds of form letter are typed each week (or month or quarter), how many of each kind, and how much time (on the average) does each letter take? How many forms, reports, proposals, résumés, and other documents have to be typed, and how long (on the average) does each take? How much of the office's typing is original typing? Retyping of a revised letter or document? Minor corrections on a nearly finished letter or document? Does any of the office's work have to be set in type?

How many meetings does the manager attend each month? How many days, on the average, does each trip take? How many meetings accomplish the result for which they were scheduled? How many must actually be face-to-face? How many interoffice memos does the manager send? How many meetings does he or she schedule each week? Are the data needed for decision making always timely, or are printouts obsolete by the time they reach the manager's desk?

In terms of the organization or office unit, what wishes do all employees have for improving individual satisfaction and achievement? Improving chances for advancement, recognition, and increased responsibility? Improving the quality of the work environment? What is their view of the organization's health in terms of absenteeism, turnover, overtime, grievances?

From the personal perspective, what kinds of work do individuals most enjoy doing? What are their strongest professional and/or technical skills? What sorts of jobs do individuals hope to hold two years from now? Five years from now?

To gather data, coordinators will use questionnaires like the ones at the end of this chapter—one to be completed by managers and one to be completed by support staff. The latter questionnaire has two main parts. One part is designed to find out how much secretarial time is devoted to various kinds of typing. The second part is designed to find out how much time is spent by the support staff in administrative and other support activities.

With the help of the consultant, the coordinator must decide what and how much data to collect. Some offices keep highly detailed data on productivity and need only extract from those data. Others have only a general idea. Collect only the data needed. For instance, if funds are limited and letters, form letters, and memos pose the office's greatest typing problem, collect data on only those kinds of typing. Forget about data on reports, proposals, forms, and the like. Also, collect data for a typical period. Try not to schedule data collection for a period when the demands are unusually high or low. However, if workload is always uneven or if the data collection must occur during a period of atypical demand, the office systems consultant can advise on how to adjust the final estimates of need.

The coordinator will collect data on *volume* (how many of each kind of typing, how long, and how much lead time does the office get), *nature of work* (letter, report, proposal, résumé, etc.), *quality* (camera ready, letter quality, rough draft), and *special features* required (such as merging of form letters with names and addresses in a data list, access to a central computer for data, super- and subscripts for equations, foreign language capability, etc.).

No matter how large the organization is, data collection should be completed within one week. The coordinator should get as much help as possible with data collection so that everyone feels involved.

Data analysis. The consultant will help the coordinator analyze the data and prepare a written report to be submitted to the unit manager. The analysis will list potential improvements such as increased number of transactions per hour, better quality of finished product, and reduced processing time. Stultz (1982) advises projecting conservatively, especially when the equipment's theoretical performance deviates from actual performance. For instance, a printer that prints 55 characters per second (CPS) works faster than a 70-word-per-minute typist. Thus, the printer will be idle much of the time unless the operator is doing much more revision than input (especially of long documents) or the printer is shared with other operators.

Analyzing costs often requires isolating the cost of specific steps in units such as the following (Stultz, 1982, pp. 166-167):

- Net units produced for each direct hour of labor.
- Keystrokes per hour.
- Minutes per office transaction, possibly broken down into minutes per specific type of transaction.
- Supply cost per net unit produced.
- Supply volume consumed per process.
- Scrap value as a percentage of sales dollars.
- Equipment depreciation or lease as a percentage of product value.
- Equipment down time.
- Number of items processed per square foot of space.
- Number of sales dollars generated per person.
- Payroll as a percentage of sales dollars.
- Material/supplies as a percentage of sales dollars.
- Inventory cost as a percentage of billable activity.
- Profit after taxes as a percentage of business assets.
- Direct labor hours or minutes per page unit.
- Indirect labor hours per direct labor hours.
- Attendance hours as a percentage of available work hours.

These standards can be converted to standard units and used as indicators in your models.

Analysis of the social system should identify potential areas of improvement such as:

- New work groups and assignments, sometimes involving job switches between personnel and sometimes involving new task assignments.
- Changed physical environments, often involving remodeling of offices.

- Training programs.
- Suggestion boxes.
- Salary studies.
- Changes in the procedure for personnel evaluation.
- Better communication to staff.

Feedback and decision. The coordinator and the office systems consultant should meet personally with the unit manager to communicate the contents of the report. The report should specify recommendations clearly. Is office automation needed? If so, what is needed most? Word processing? Message switching? Calendar keeping? And how much or what kind is needed? Third, what is the degree of organizational acceptance?

The report should be honest, with all facts checked out. It should contain quantitative documentation with specific models and comparison sheets that show clearly how a new system would be superior to the old one. In most cases the report should show payback in 18 to 36 months or sooner (Goldfield, 1980a). The faster the payback, the better.

Stultz (1982, pp. 173-174) recommends having on hand analyses of alternate systems to back up the recommendation. The report will be much more convincing if the presenter can answer questions with, say, "Yes, we considered System C, but turnaround would be half a day slower, and payback would take 3½ years." In some cases the consultant and coordinator will have used a weighting technique, such as the one explained in Chapter 6, to aid in making a choice.

The proposed solution should describe the relationship between the inputs, tasks, technologies, and outputs. Each operation/function should be flowcharted in terms of origination, production, reproduction, storage, distribution, and control. The report should also speak to the possible contribution to an operation of special technologies such as telecommunications.

The report must give the manager enough information to enable him or her to answer several general questions. For instance, if the report proposes word processing equipment as the backbone application, the manager will need to know the answers to the following questions:

- What kinds of office work should go on a word processor? Form letters only? All letters? All letters and résumés? Or everything? In other words, decide the scope of the work to be word processed.
- What benefits are desired? Is the goal to be able to handle the current workload without hiring additional staff? To reduce staff size? To be able to add value to current services?
- Does the department have funds adequate to pay for a word processor?
- What limits exist? For instance, space might be too cramped to accommodate equipment, or funds insufficient. If staff turnover is

unusually high, the word processor should be one on which training will be quick and easy.

- What criteria will be used to evaluate the word processor after it has been in use for a time? Some criteria will relate directly to the benefits hoped for. Others might have to do with quality and quantity of work produced, cost per unit of work, turnaround time for each kind of typing, staff morale, and so forth.

If the proposal is for executive support systems, the report will have to contain information on topics such as the following:

- How many person-hours will be saved? For executives? For support staff? For instance, by one estimate (Marcus, 1980), electronic mail could save professionals up to two hours per day.
- How many fewer days will executives spend traveling? How much money will be saved in travel costs?

With executive support systems, though, facts are harder to quantify because the emphasis is on value added rather than on cost displacement. The latter emphasizes improving the efficiency of current production so that real time and money can be saved. In contrast, "value added" refers to the ability to perform more, new, better, or more timely work. In addition, value can increase an individual's capacity or worth to an organization. These concepts are hard to quantify.

How, for instance, do we quantify Don Ragle's (Chapter 2 vignette) ability to supervise more closely, preventing problems before they arise? How do we evaluate his ability to find time to visit the dentist *before* an aching tooth causes him to take sick time? To call up additional data to answer a question raised in a teleconference, enabling a decision on the spot without another meeting (Chapter 6 vignette)? We can quantify the travel days saved; we have no way to quantify the savings in executive thinking time. Feidelman (1981) argues persuasively that the top-down approach, beginning with executives, is often a highly efficient way to start automation.

Lodahl (1980), who has done content analysis on the "new" work created by executives with support systems, has found that on the whole, the new work is at least as valuable as that being done before. When he put a value on the new work, Lodahl was able to estimate a value-added average of $10,000 per professional per year.

Develop a general time-action plan. If automation is recommended, the coordinator and the office systems consultant should reach a general agreement on the nature and time line of a plan for action.

The next step is to lay out a detailed plan of implementation. The plan must describe how the technical and social systems of the work unit will function as a result of the new technology. At the end of this chapter is a summary of the topics described in the paragraphs that follow. Many managers and coordinators may want to use it as a guideline for preparing their final report and recommendations.

Definition of project.   Place boundaries around the project. Different people will perceive the project differently. Consequently, managers must develop a common framework for members of a unit to use in viewing the project. The coordinator, perhaps working with a task force, needs to define the project objectives in specific, measurable terms. The coordinator and task force must also identify the tasks that will be automated and those that will, at least for the time being, continue to be performed in the traditional way.

The coordinator and task force must also state performance requirements (e.g., "we want each operator to be able to produce ___ letters per day") and requirements for special equipment, such as back-up document storage. Hold information meetings for everyone who will be affected by the plans.

Benefits to be achieved.   Benefits are both tangible and intangible. The models developed earlier will help the task force or the coordinator to put a dollar value on different areas of automation. In general, the larger the workload in an area, the greater the potential dollar savings.

Intangible benefits, which must also be spelled out, include factors such as improvement in service, quality, and control. For secretaries, these benefits may include (Goldfield, 1980a):

- The reduction or elimination of boring or repetitive tasks.
- The automation of mindless office jobs.
- Improved career opportunities.
- Increased pay scales.
- The chance to develop new skills.

For corporations as a whole, the intangible but specific benefits from automation have included (Marcus, 1980, p. 12):

- Decentralized opportunity for initiative and creativity by having terminals at most professional and secretarial desks.
- More timely creation of work to address opportunities.
- More timely communication to staff in other locations.
- Greater use of interactive graphics to show trends in data.
- Better working relationships because of teleconferencing and electronic mail.

More general benefits include:

- Staff members' sense of belonging to a progressive, forward-looking organization.
- More time for challenging analyses and decision making.
- Increased initiative and creativity, leading to chances for self-actualization and a more satisfied work force (refer to the vignettes at the beginning of this chapter).
- Reduction of lengthy work hours through increased efficiency and time savings (compare Alex Zellar's and Don Ragle's days, Chapter 2).
- Flexibility that allows working at home when necessary.

Organizational design. The coordinator of the task force needs to lay out the proposed office structure to identify all places where people and technology will interface. (The next section discusses major office structures.) This analysis helps to point out positions that can be eliminated, jobs that will change, people who will need training, and so forth.

Choosing an Office Structure

People and machines get along together best when office organization takes into account people's needs, and office layout is an important aspect of organization. Briefly, the four basic layouts focus on word processing centers, administrative support teams, individual secretaries, and key operators, respectively. Sometimes the best arrangement combines the basic layouts, which are described briefly below.

For help in planning the physical layout of offices, consult articles such as Prince's (1980) "Environments that Work for People" and "Open Plan Complements a Conventional Space" (no author, 1980). (This and other helpful articles are reviewed in the annotated bibliography.)

Word processing centers. A word processing center consists of one or more work stations located in one central area. Unless the office has previously included a typing pool, the establishment of a center represents a significant change. Work can be organized in one of two ways.

1. A dedicated staff of typists may do all entry on the word processors. These typists would have few, if any, administrative functions. This scheme maximizes use of the processor and reduces the amount of time needed to teach personnel how to use the processor.

2. The second way is to have all secretaries use the center. Under this scheme secretaries retain their administrative functions, leaving their stations when they need to use the processor. This scheme requires no personnel changes but *does* require training all

secretaries. It also requires secretaries to leave their normal stations unattended while using the word processor.

Managers attracted to the idea of centralized word processing should take caution from Stanford University's experience (Marcus, 1980, p. 6). In February 1980 Stanford abandoned an institution-wide center because it had lost cost effectiveness. The center's physical distance from many campus offices and the lack of ultimate control over departmental work production dissuaded many from using the service.

Administrative support team. An administrative support team might have several work stations in a localized area that provides administrative and typing support for a specific group of authors. This form of organization requires relatively few changes in personnel and office environment. Each secretary receives a station and learns how to use it, and no secretary has to leave the work station to do typing. However, unless the office has either (1) a high volume of work eligible for word processing or (2) support systems such as electronic mail, message switching, and scheduling, an administrative cluster might be quite expensive and hard to justify.

Individual secretaries. When each secretary has a work station, he or she can perform administrative and typing functions without restrictions. Again, though, unless the volume of typing is high or support systems are being used, the cost can be prohibitive.

Key operators. Key operators are mainly word processing operators, but they do not work in a pool. Instead, they are part of an administrative support team and are physically located with the team.

Combination arrangement. Combinations can be structured in many ways. For instance, suppose you want to set up a word processing center and rearrange managers and support staff into administrative support centers, but the managers object to losing their private secretaries. One possible solution is to set up a small word processing center with an OCR device. Let secretaries continue to type first drafts on their typewriters. Let the scanner read the drafts into the word processors for revision. Gradually change the staff structure as either secretaries or managers resign, forming first one support center and then another, gradually enlarging the WP center as needed to accommodate the larger work load.

Fitting People to Roles

The coordinator or the task force, working with the manager, will need to examine staff members' skills and preferences to match individuals with the reorganized jobs that best suit them. Excellent typists who don't like being interrupted by telephones and who don't fear technology will probably make excellent word processing operators. Secretaries who like nontyping work best probably will make excellent administrative support secretaries. Consider any writers on the staff. Some would be delighted to have their own entry terminal (and you'll have the pleasure of watching their productivity double or triple). Others won't want anything to do with the new system.

Consider the administrators. Those with computer skills may want their own terminals and may prove to be strong allies for automation. Identify those who prefer dictating to a private secretary. They'll need training in how to use dictation equipment. Some, as Scannell (1980a, 1980b) warns, will balk at any change in the status quo. Remember that you can't predict managers' attitudes from their age. Some older managers will be strong supporters of automation, and some younger ones will be strong resisters.

With tact and careful planning, though, planners will be able to persuade all staff to make the needed changes. If the coordinator is farsighted enough, he or she will have managed to entice one or two reluctant staff members onto the task force and the experience will have helped them to adjust. They, in turn, will help to persuade others as reluctant as they once were.

Summary

The analysis of objectives, costs, benefits, and impacts on people should result in a firm, detailed implementation plan that the task force "owns" and that the coordinator and task force can present to the manager.

IMPLEMENTATION

Implementation involves planning to help people adjust to role changes. It involves preparation of the facility, initial training, planning of procedures and policies, and actual installation.

Announcement of Changes

When a plan has been approved, announce the plan and the time frame. Fear of the unknown always inspires resistance to change, so defuse that issue by providing knowledge. Some people will be eager for change. Others won't be and will feel that the change is going to change their work for the worse. Hold another meeting for all who will be affected by the plans. It is best to get objections and resistance out into the open before implementation actually occurs.

Staff and administrators' attitudes play a big part in whether word processors accomplish the tasks expected of them. Effectiveness can be sabotaged by employees who sneak back to the friendly, comfortable typewriter whenever possible. Some secretaries, distrustful of mailing label programs, have hidden away their addressograph plates and use them instead whenever possible, even though it means hand typing all addresses added since the use of the plates was officially discontinued!

Tales like this shouldn't discourage you, only make you aware that at no stage in the process can you ignore people. From the very beginning, share your information about word processing with everyone in the office. If possible, arrange with the office coordinator to take staff members for informal demonstrations of what word processors can accomplish. Secretaries who are tired of typing form letters over and over but afraid of dealing with "data files" (of names and addresses) find their fear disappearing when they watch another secretary build a data file and dispatch 85 form letters in less than two hours.

Buy or borrow copies of magazines on word processing and modern office systems. Chapter 3 contains suggestions.

Preparation for Installation

Begin preparation by making a list of all repairs, additions, remodeling, and service connections that have to be made before the word processor can be installed. For instance, with a shared system, identify all offices that must have a cable laid between them and the central processor. If the central processor requires air conditioning and special arrangements for ventilation, arrange for both well in advance. If offices must be rearranged and lighting changed, plan for that. Don't expect your first list to be the final one. As people work through the list, other essential tasks will surface and require tending. Simply add those to your list. For help, see Chapter 4. Check your list with a qualified architect, facilities engineer, or buildings and grounds department.

Work like this can take longer than it will take the equipment to arrive, so get as early a start as possible and "bird-dog" the people responsible for getting the work done. You don't want your processor sitting uselessly in crates in the hall!

Next, check the furniture in the office with the requirements of the new equipment. Make a list of furniture needed and furniture you'll no longer need. When you make the furniture list, keep in mind any structural and organizational changes you are making in the office because those will affect your furniture needs.

Before designing work stations, read Al Schumann's (1981) helpful article on "How to Develop a Useful Work Station Analysis," which gives detailed instructions on how to construct comfortable, appropriate work stations.

Reread the vendor's material on equipment requirements for items you might not think about. For instance, sound hoods for impact printers can quiet an office and contribute to the well-being of staff members. (Recent research has shown that constant sound, even at supposedly nondangerous levels, contributes to nervous stress and irritability.) Static mats on the floor will keep ordinary movement from generating static that scrambles the writing on a CRT.

If you have arranged to have the vendor convert documents by optical scanning, now is the time to get the process started.

Initial Training

Plan on initial training for supervisors, regular operators, back-up operators, and managers. Choose the word processing staff—supervisor (if you need one), regular operators, and backup operators. If possible, arrange with the vendor for initial training. You should know, from prepurchase investigation, what training arrangements are available and how much they cost, but now is the time to choose the specific arrangement that suits your office. If additional cost is involved, get approval for that.

Find out where the training will take place—in your office or the vendor's. If the latter, try to schedule it for the first day or two after the equipment has been installed and is working. That way, newly trained staff won't lose the benefits of training by having a delay between the date of training and the date of first use. Find out about and arrange for follow-up training and extended training, on-site support during the start-up period, and training manuals. As a rule, purchasers of microcomputers with word processing software will get little or no training.

Training for managers is crucial, particularly for those who have always originated documents by dictating to a personal secretary. Many executives resist machine dictating, in part because they've not been taught how to manage the equipment. It's easy to ask Ms. Jones to read back what you've just said. Many managers fear learning how to make a machine do the same thing. However, as the vignettes in Chapter 2 show, dictating to a private secretary takes up two people's time. Dictating and word processing combined can effect great savings, increase productivity, and raise quality *if* staff will use them. When you study the needs of your organization, look for signs of resistance to dictation. If you find it, include in your plans dictation training for managers and executives at all levels. Teaching techniques and explaining reasons will help to reduce resistance. One helpful resource is the IWP's (n.d.) *Command Dictation Manual,* available free to IWP members.

Identify supplies you'll need and place orders. A starting list of items is:

- Diskettes and/or backup disk.
- Continuous-form paper, which comes in several sizes. Some offices want 8½ by 11 paper including the holes that attach the paper to the tractor, or pins, on the printer. Others want paper with snap-off sides that leaves an 8½ by 11 page *after* the sides have been snapped off. That paper is size 9 by 11.
- Print wheels.
- Ribbons.
- Mailing labels.

We suggest a six-week supply. When doing this task, find out the sources of all these supplies and establish procedures for reordering. Also find out how long it will take from placement of order to delivery.

Procedures

The products you purchase will come with instructions, but your organization will have to design and document its own internal procedures. Eventually this task will be taken over by the office support group (described in Chapter 8), but at planning time the responsibility rests with the office systems consultant and the coordinator, who will need to keep systematic notes on decisions as they are made. Help for this task can be found in Cecil's (1980) article, "Write Your Own Word Processing Manual."

The staff you now have won't always be with you, so plan for *ongoing replacement and training.* Staff members will sometimes be ill or on vacation, so plan for *back-up help.* One helpful approach is the mobile operator concept described in Hedden's (1981) article, "The Mobile Operator Concept in Corporate Word Processing."

Design *work request forms* that reflect the capabilities of the new equipment and your plan for *management of priorities.*

Plan for *document cataloging and referencing.* Think about the categories of work done, the substantive topics involved, the different organizational parts of your office, and the people who are doing the work. Try to devise a system for document naming that everyone will use and that will make recall as easy as possible, even when a creating operator is no longer employed by your office.

Establish procedures for *"archiving"*—maintaining historical copies of old files. If your system has a hard disk, you'll need to plan system purging procedures to prevent the disk from becoming too full to operate. Put in writing which files are to be destroyed ("purged," or erased) after use. For instance, you might keep a paper copy of one-time letters for six months and target the electronic copy for either immediate destruction or destruction as of a specific date. Whatever the procedures, put them in writing and make sure everyone has a copy.

Establish procedures for *originating and revising* documents. If necessary, train all writers in dictation procedures and procedures for marking corrections on drafts. Also establish associated *quality control* procedures and be sure word originators understand them. With the higher quality of typing that word processing makes available, will some writers begin demanding higher quality simply because they can get it, and would that demand cut into your anticipated productivity increases? Some offices have found that writers who once tolerated a few hand-written corrections now insist on typed corrections and retyping. Both are easy to do, but if enough people want this service, your office could find itself producing little more than before, although at much higher quality. Furthermore, when word originators discover how easy new drafts are, they often feel freer to be sloppy with original proofreading because if they catch a mistake later, it can always be corrected easily. True, corrections are easy, but repeated correction and printing of the same document wastes everyone's time. Establish guidelines that will help operators know when to refuse such requests. You may need to remind some people that a small handwritten correction that was acceptable on a hand-typed letter is just as acceptable on a word processed letter.

An innovative secretary in one of our research offices, which produced many long documents, devised a system that enlists peer pressure to keep demanding users in line. The office has a blackboard on which writers list their jobs with name, due date, and desired priority. Every user and staff member can see the board and recognize repeated requests for work on the same document, repeated "rush" requests by the same user, and the like.

Another possibility, for offices with several work stations, is to require writers to do their own minor corrections.

Closely related to these efforts is the need for procedures to keep a smooth *work flow* in the office. You'll need to devise a master plan for both input terminals and printers to integrate rush jobs with long reports, batches of form letters, ordinary correspondence, and so forth. If rush jobs are a fact of life in your firm, you may find it helpful to consult Steinbrecher's (1980) article, "When Time is the Only Consideration, Then the Only Way is RUSH."

Other preparations should include the following:

- Establishing procedures to *measure productivity*. Helpful articles are Hanson's (1981) on measurement standards and Watkins' (1981) on performance indicators.

- Establishing procedures for *performance evaluation* of personnel.
- *Revising job descriptions* to take into account word processing responsibilities.
- Establishing *backup procedures* to protect each day's work.
- Establishing procedures for *starting up and shutting down* each day; and integrating these procedures with backup procedures.
- Establishing *accounting procedures* so that the proper account is charged for each piece of work done.

POST-AUDIT

After the system has been installed, take time for an evaluation. If possible have two audits: one by the organization's internal auditor and one by an independent team. Assess whether the operators were properly and thoroughly trained. (If not, discuss the situation with the vendor.) Measure productivity and compare levels with previous levels and expected levels as shown in your models. Evaluate the changes in office structure. Evaluate the office's achievements in terms of the objectives you set when you studied office needs. Are those objectives being met? As benchmark guidelines, use the detailed objectives and benefits listed in the detailed implementation plan.

Finally, plan for the future. You'll want to measure productivity and work level at regular intervals to find out what the growth rate is so you can plan for expansion, if necessary, well in advance.

REPORT FORMAT
DESCRIPTION OF A PROJECT

Project Objectives

Describe main objectives in specific, measurable terms. Identify objectives designed to achieve cost efficiency and objectives designed to add value to the organization's services. For instance:

Cost Savings

- WP equipment should reduce staff overhead by tripling the output per typist.
- WP equipment should improve document preparation by reducing turnaround time from one week to two days.
- Electronic mail and message switching should reduce postage costs by 40%.

QUESTIONNAIRE FOR MANAGERS

General Information

Name: _____ Dept: _____

Title: _____ Date: _____

Names of support staff who do your typing: _____

_____

1. In the office, how do you create work to be typed? Longhand ____% Short-hand ____% Machine dictation ____% Self-typed ____%

2. Do you create typing work away from the office? Y/N If yes, how often? _____ _____ How do you generate this work?

   Longhand ____% Shorthand ____% Machine dict. ____% Self-typed ____%

3. Do you ever ask for rough drafts? Y/N If yes, (what) ____% of total typed material? Why?

4. Do you ever wish you could revise finished material but do not because of a deadline? Y/N

5. Do you have peak periods? Y/N When do they occur?

6. How often does your typing end up backlogged?

   Frequently ____ Occasionally ____ Never ____

7. Are you satisfied with the appearance of the documents leaving your office? Y/N

8. Are you now performing any administrative tasks that could be delegated to a secretary if the time were available? Y/N If yes:

   Copying Y/N Composing Y/N Filing Y/N Sorting Y/N
   Research Y/N Posting and bookkeeping Y/N Other _____

9. Is there work you want done that is not currently being done? Y/N

10. Do you anticipate personnel changes in the next 6–12 months? Y/N If yes, what kinds of change? _____

_____

Correspondence

1. How do you create correspondence? Longhand ____% Shorthand ____% Machine dictation ____% Self-typed ____%

2. How long do you create correspondence each day? Less than 1 hour per day ____ 1–3 hours/day ____ 3–5 hours/day ____

3. Do you originate correspondence away from the office? Y/N If yes, how often? _____

4. Do you ever ask for rough drafts of correspondence? Y/N If yes, for what percentage of total correspondence? Less than 15% ____ 15–25% ____ 25–50% ____ More than 50% ____

5. Do you ever revise letters that are delivered to you in "finished" form? Y/N If yes, how often? ____ times per day.

6. How long does it take to get your letters typed? Less than 1 day ____ About 2 days ____ More than 2 days ____

7. Do you send out original repetitive letters? Y/N

8. Do you send out form letters with fill-ins? Y/N

9. Do you compose letters that include "standard," "stock," or "boilerplate" paragraphs? Y/N

Long Documents

1. How do you create long documents? Longhand ____% Shorthand ____% Machine dictation ____%

2. How often do you create long documents? Weekly/Monthly/Rarely

3. Do you originate any of these documents away from the office? Y/N If yes, how often? ____ times per day/ week/ month/ year.

   How do you generate these documents? Longhand ____% Shorthand ____% Machine dictation ____% Self-typed ____%

4. Do you ever ask for rough drafts of these documents? Y/N If yes, how often? ____% of total material.

5. Do you ever change documents that are sent to you in "finished" form? Y/N If yes, how often? _____ Why? _____

6. How long does it take to get your documents typed? Less than 1 day ____ About 2 days ____ More than 2 days ____

7. Do you send out form documents with fill-ins? Y/N

8. Do you compose documents that include "standard" or "stock" paragraphs? Y/N

Communications

Interoffice Memos

1. How do you create memos? Longhand ____% Shorthand ____% Machine dictation ____% Self-typed ____%

2. How long do you create memos each day? Less than 1 hour/day ____ 1–3 hours/day ____ 3–5 hours/day ____ More ____

3. Do you originate memos away from the office? Y/N If yes, how often? _____

4. Do you ever ask for rough drafts of memos? Y/N If yes, what percentage of total correspondence? Less that 15% ____ 15–25% ____ 25–50% ____ More than 50% ____

5. Do you ever revise memos that came to you in "finished" form? Y/N If yes, how many times per day? 1–3 ____ 3–5 ____ 5–10 ____ More ____

6. How long does it take to get memos typed? Less than 1 day ____ About 2 days ____ More than 2 days ____

7. How long are your memos? Less than 1/2 page ____ One page ____ Longer ____

Meetings

1. How many meetings do you attend each week? Fewer than 5 ___ 5–10 ___ 10–15 ___ More ___

1. Of these meetings, how many are in town but not in your building? Fewer than 5 ___ 5–10 ___ 10–15 ___ More ___

1. Of these meetings, how many require travel to an out-of-town location? Fewer than 5 ___ 5–10 ___ 10–15 ___ More ___

2. On the average, how long do meetings last? Less than 1 hour/meeting ___ 1–3 hours/mtg ___ 3–5 hours/mtg ___

3. On the average, how many days each week are you away from the office? None ___ 1–2 ___ 3–4 ___ More ___

4. On the average, how many meetings accomplish the result you intended? Less than 25% ___ 25–50% ___ 50–75% ___ More ___

5. Is lack of data ever a reason why meetings don't accomplish your goal? Y/N If yes, how many times/week? 1–3 ___ 3–5 ___ 5–10 ___ More ___

6. Are there other reasons?

7. Do you or your secretary have to schedule meetings? Y/N If yes, how many times per week? 1–3 ___ 3–5 ___ 5–10 ___ More ___

8. On the average, how long does it take to schedule a meeting and confirm all attendees? 1–3 hours ___ 3–5 hours ___ Longer ___

Records Management

1. Do you use typed or handwritten lists of records? Y/N If no, do you get such lists from the data processing section?

2. Describe the purpose of each list or record name.

3. How often do you need access to any of these lists or records? Daily/ Weekly/ Monthly/ Infrequently

4. Do you maintain these lists or records? Y/N If no, who maintains them?

5. Would you expand your use of lists or records if time and/or resources allowed? Y/N

Data Processing

1. Do you use information stored on a computer? Y/N If no, move to "Comments" section (below).

2. Where is the computer located? _____

3. Do you use a display terminal to access data? Y/N

4. Does your staff use display terminal to access data? Y/N

5. Describe the types of information you currently get from computer outputs. _____
   _____
   _____

6. Do you foresee a need to access additional data stored on a computer?   Y/N

7. What percentage of data is presented to you via: ____% printout ____% retyped or reformatted ____% merged with other material?

8. Is the data that reaches your desk timely? Always ____ Most of the time ____ Some of the time ____ Nearly always out of date ____

Evaluation of Organization and Work Environment

1. What wishes do you have for your organization or job unit that would:

   A. Improve individual employee satisfaction and achievement?

   _____

   _____

   _____

   B. Improve chances for advancement, recognition, and increased responsibility?

   _____

   _____

   _____

   C. Improve the organization's or unit's chances to attain its goals?

   _____

   _____

   _____

   D. Improve the quality of the work environment?

   _____

   _____

   _____

2. Are you satisfied with your current level of staff support?   Y/N

3. If no, what improvements would you like to make in office operations?

   _____

   _____

   _____

4. What is your assessment of organizational health in terms of:

   A. Absenteeism?

   _____

   _____

   B. Turnover?

   _____

   _____

C. Overtime?

_____

_____

D. Grievances?

_____

5. How adaptive are the staff to new activities and responsibilities?

_____

_____

6. What changes would you make to improve integration of the organization's or unit's activities?

_____

_____

Evaluation of Personal Abilities and Skills

1. What kind of work do you most enjoy doing? Why?

_____

_____

2. In your judgment, what are your strongest professional and/or technical skills?

_____

_____

3. What sort of job do you hope to hold two years from now? Why?

_____

_____

4. What sort of job do you hope to hold five years from now? Why?

_____

_____

Additional comments: _____

_____

_____

_____

_____

JOB ANALYSIS: SUPPORT ACTIVITIES

Administration

Name: _____ Dept: _____

Title: _____ Typewriter make: _____

Location: _____ Pica / Elite / Executive

Managers Supported	Title	Typing Hrs/Day	Admin. Hrs/Day
_____	_____		
_____	_____		
_____	_____		
_____	_____		

During an average day, how much time do you spend doing each of the following activities? Include personal time and time you spend waiting for work. When you're done, the total amount of time should equal the total number of hours at work each day.

Administrative Duties	Hours per Day
Sorting/handling mail	_____
Telephone calls	_____
Scheduling meetings	_____
Taking shorthand dictation	_____
Filing	_____
Reproduction work	_____
Business errands, message delivery	_____
Clerical posting, recordkeeping, calculations	_____
Personal service (coffee, watering plants, etc.)	_____
Other (include special projects; describe)	_____
TOTAL	_____
Typing hours total	_____
Waiting-for-work time	_____
Personal time	_____
TOTAL HOURS/DAY	_____

List nonroutine work, such as special reports and projects, that you perform occasionally or once a week, month, or year. List the managers for whom this work is performed and the frequency (weekly, etc.), and estimate the number of hours per project.

Managers	Type of Project	Frequency	Hrs/Project

Describe briefly the nature of your job and how your managers work. If there are special work situations, such as much travel or peaks and valleys in work flow, describe them here.

_____

_____

_____

_____

_____

Typing

Name: _____ Department: _____

1. Is typing your primary job function?   Y/N

2. What kind of typewriter do you use? Electric/Manual; brand name is _____

3. Is it located at your desk?   Y/N

4. How much of your typing is rough draft? 10% / 25% / 50% / 75%

5. What amount of revision is necessary to the documents you type? Please indicate percentage distribution to:

    ____ None   ____ Light; occasional change in word or sentence

    ____ Moderate

    ____ Very heavy; often add new charts and paragraphs; often move paragraphs from one page to another

6. Is typing ever revised more than one time?   Y/N

7. How is the typing work given to you? Please indicate percentage distribution to:

    ____ Longhand   ____ Shorthand

    ____ Machine dictation   ____ Previously typed copy

    ____ Self-composition   ____ Other (please describe)

8. Does work come in peak periods at certain times of the year?   Y/N
   If yes, when? _____

9. Normal deadline requirements: Same day / One day / Two days

10. Are erasures prohibited in any of the typing you do?   Y/N
    If yes, in what work? _____

11. Number of carbons normally required: ____

12. Do any of the people you work for travel?   Y/N

13. Do you have to work overtime?   Y/N   If yes, how many hours per week? ____

14. Do you use transcription equipment?   Y/N   If yes, brand name is _____

15. Do you use a copy machine? Y/N If yes, how far is it from your desk? Same floor / Different floor _____ If different floor, give floor number ____.

16. Do you often have to wait in line at the copier?   Y/N   If yes, how long? 1–2 minutes 3–5 minutes / longer

17. Are you required to maintain lists or records that are not stored on a computer?   Y/N   If yes, please describe the purpose of each list or record.

    How many hours per week, on the average, are required to maintain these lists or files? ____ hours

    Do you retype the information for use in other documents?   Y/N

18. How often does your office use (give percentage distribution):

    ____Letterhead   ____Bond

    ____Printed forms   ____Stencils

    ____Multiple-part forms or paper

    (Please attach samples of all forms.)

19. For a typical work week, indicate by percentage of total typing the amount of typing you do that involves:

    Time period is:

    This is (is not) a typical workload.

    (If atypical) What is not typical?

    ____% Memoranda or internal letters
    ____% Letters outside the firm
    ____% Narrative reports; multiple-page documents, such as reports and proposals, longer than two typed pages
    ____% Matter that is to be published
    ____% Statistical typing; columnar format
    ____% Outlines; typing jobs of any length that require the use of indented or outline format
    ____% Repetitive typing or fill-in letters; letters and other correspondence items that are individually addressed but either reused or done from "standard" or "stock" paragraphs
    ____% Text with tables of information
    ____% Forms fill-ins; preprinted documents
    ____% Technical typing: specifications, procedures, or documentation
    ____% Transcription; meeting reports or medical reports
    ____% Scientific notation; contains chemical radicals, Greek symbols, sub- and superscripts
    ____% Rough draft typing
    ____% Miscellaneous

_____ Envelopes
_____ Index cards
_____ Labels
_____% Other (please specify)
_____
_____
_____

20. Do you have special requirements for paper size? If so, what are they?

21. Do you ever have typed information printed and/or duplicated by a printer? If so, what? How many volumes?

22. Do you use data stored on a computer? Y/N If yes, what data on which computers?

23. Do you retype this information? Never/ Sometimes/ Always

24. Do you see a future need for access to computerized data? If so, what, when, and to which computers?

Evaluation of Organization and Work Environment

1. What wishes do you have for your organization or job unit that would:

A. Improve individual employee satisfaction and achievement?

_____
_____
_____

B. Improve chances for advancement, recognition, and increased responsibility?

_____
_____
_____

C. Improve the organization's or unit's chances to attain its goals?

_____
_____
_____

D. Improve the quality of the work environment?

_____
_____
_____

2. If the answer to D is no, what improvements would you like to make in office operations?

_____
_____
_____

3. What is your assessment of organizational health in terms of:

   A. Absenteeism?

   _____

   _____

   B. Turnover?

   _____

   _____

   C. Overtime?

   _____

   _____

   D. Grievances?

   _____

   _____

4. How adaptive are the staff to new activities and responsibilities?

   _____

   _____

   _____

5. What changes would you make to improve integration of the organization's or unit's activities?

   _____

   _____

   _____

Evaluation of Personal Abilities and Skills

1. What kind of work do you most enjoy doing? Why?

   _____

   _____

   _____

2. In your judgment, what are your strongest professional and/or technical skills?

   _____

   _____

   _____

3. What sort of job do you hope to hold two years from now? Why?

   _____

   _____

   _____

4. What sort of job do you hope to hold five years from now? Why?

_____

_____

_____

Additional Comments

_____

_____

_____

_____

_____

_____

_____

_____

_____

_____

_____

_____

_____

_____

_____

_____

_____

_____

_____

_____

_____

_____

_____

- Teleconferencing should reduce executive travel time to three days per month or fewer.
- Executive support system should reduce typing of interoffice memos by 80%.

Distinguish between objectives to be addressed by technical change and objectives to be achieved through redesign of jobs or organizational change. For instance, the last three objectives listed above would be achieved through technical change; the first two, through a combination of organizational and technical change. List objectives in order of importance.

System Applications

List processes to be automated in order of importance. For instance:

- Maintain address files for prospective buyers.
- Maintain list of job applicants; merge with announcement letter.
- Maintain résumés.
- Maintain frequently-used paragraphs of text (boilerplate) and abbreviated résumés for proposals.

Also identify and list processes that are to be maintained manually.

Requirements for Equipment Performance

List performance requirements that the equipment must meet in order to be useful. Be specific and quantitative. For instance:

- Response time for document access must not exceed 2.5 seconds.
- Back-up procedures must not take more than 30 minutes per day.
- Printer must be able to turn out up to 350 letters per day.
- Breakdowns must not stop work for more than 4 hours.

Document Storage Requirements

List requirements for document storage with respect to availability, security, and selectivity. Specifically:

- *Document availability:* What will be the relationship between age and availability of documents? For instance, will it be acceptable to take a day to give users access to a document that hasn't been used for two months?
- *Document security:* What, if any, security restrictions are needed? Should anyone be allowed to ask for any document? Or should certain categories be restricted?

- *Document selectivity:* What will be the normal procedure for retrieving documents?

ANTICIPATED BENEFITS FROM OFFICE SYSTEMS PROJECT

Identify tangible benefits such as cost savings. Count not only actual anticipated reductions but the ability to handle larger workloads without additional personnel, facilities, or expenses. Calculate a dollar value for these benefits.

Also identify intangible benefits such as improved service, better control of quality, and so forth.

ALTERNATIVES

If the chosen solution was one of several possibilities, briefly discuss the other solutions and summarize differences in a table. Give the reasons for rejecting each alternative.

DESCRIPTION OF OFFICE SYSTEM

If the report contains more than one possible way to organize an office system, discuss the chosen alternative first. Arrange discussion of the others to emphasize their differences from the preferred solution. The discussion should contain:

- *Narrative description* of office system. Include the basic characteristics of the system including new technologies, job redesigns, and organizational changes.
- *Functions.* Describe in terms of the proposed system.
- *Limitations.* List functions, features, and capabilities that others may expect to find covered but that aren't, in fact, included in the proposed system. If the system will be installed in phases, with each phase expanding the capabilities, specify the limitations for each phase.
- *Design.* Diagram how the system will be organized.
- *Inputs and data entry.* Specify any special actions that users will have to take to enter documents or data. Include specifications for use of dictation equipment, data collection forms, OCR font typewriters, and so forth.
- *Principal files.* List the principal files of the system with their general contents and intended file use. Include document files and list and records management files.
- *Outputs.* If special outputs will be available, such as reduced-size typing or intelligent copier output, describe how to use them and include samples.
- *Special design requirements.* Identify any applications that require special development. For instance, management of many complex

mailing lists will require special development. So would a bank of marketing survey questions from which researchers might want to use only a few at any one time.

- *Teleprocessing considerations.* Describe any proposed communications links, including main characteristics and requirements.
- *Controls.* Describe office systems procedures to ensure the integrity and security of the system. Describe password control, other security measures (if any), and routines for "archiving," or storing, old documents.
- *Organizational changes.* Identify and describe any changes in the structure of the work unit including reporting lines, personnel role changes, and physical layout of the office.

ANALYSIS OF DATA

Compare the proposed solution with the organization's master plan of goals and objectives. Compare benefits from each alternative with the objectives for office automation. Compare costs of alternatives. List planned quantities of equipment, models, and any other information needed to prepare a purchase request. Specify target dates for installation along with a list of any conditions that might prevent meeting the dates.

SUPPORTING DATA AND APPENDIXES

Most firms will want to include a glossary with definitions of key terms such as those in Chapter 3. Organize the abbreviations alphabetically and highlight any abbreviations used in the document. Include any supporting papers needed to document the reasons for decisions.

On-Going Support
For Modern
8 Office Technology

Modern office technology needs on-going operational support. In some small businesses, an interested owner or employee will work with the vendor to provide support. Others will want to work out an agreement to have the vendor provide some support. Large firms will want to maintain an office systems support unit. The structure and size of the unit depend on a firm's size and style of management. Size also depends on degree of automation. The greater the amount of equipment installed, the larger the office systems support unit will need to be.

This chapter discusses the services needed and describes a form of organization and services suitable to medium to large firms. The assumption is that such firms will be served by large shared-logic or time-shared systems. Specifically, we suggest that an office systems team include expertise on data and word processing, telecommunications, reproduction, and records management. Team members help managers throughout a firm with the complex tasks of applying new technologies to labor-intensive activities. Without this team, each department would tend to duplicate the specialized

skills or the technology. The result usually is both higher costs and incompatibility of technology among departments. Figure 8.1 shows the functional design for an office systems unit.

CUSTOMER SUPPORT

An office systems unit must provide service equal to or better than that a vendor would provide. In particular, the equipment and the service must perform better than a stand-alone unit serviced by a vendor. Anything less will cause grumbling in the offices and possibly even rejection. Service should begin with preinstallation consulting and planning, coordination of installation, and co-ordination among user groups.

Consultation

Office systems consultants provide the technical knowledge that most office managers lack. They help managers define their needs and put together the services needed with the technologies that are available. Consultants help to coordinate technologies to prevent incompatibilities from preventing gains in productivity.

Consultants can either do the work themselves or coach others, such as the coordinators discussed in Chapter 7, who are doing the work. Either way, data collection occurs through tools and techniques like those discussed in Chapter 7. The data can be either hard (e.g., how many letters do you type each day?) or soft (e.g., what are your goals for the office?). A needs assessment results in specific recommendations.

Once a recommendation has been accepted, offices often need consultation on planning for implementation, training, and applications.

Preinstallation Planning

Preinstallation planning maximizes the effectiveness of the new technology. Consultants, working with a coordinator or unit manager, configure the technical system to meet an office unit's needs and recommend the organizational design and personnel assignments that will be most effective in carrying out the work. Failing to make these plans only disrupts an office and dissipates gains in productivity.

Coordination of Installation

Coordination shortens the time between the decision to automate and the actual production. As Chapter 7 points out, the consultant, often working with a coordinator or manager, must list, coordinate,

119

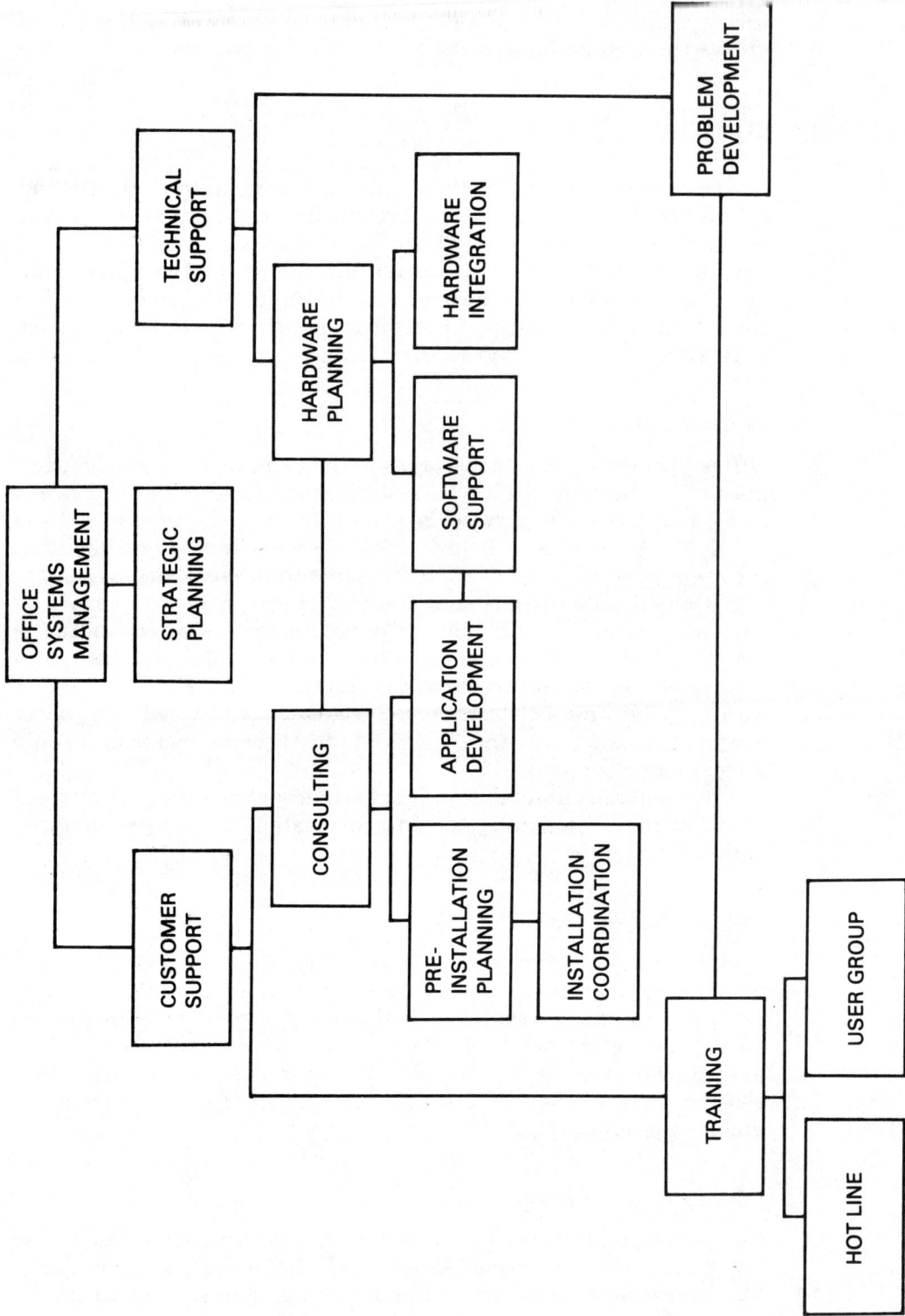

Figure 8.1 Office Systems Support

and "bird dog" preinstallation tasks such as installing wiring and air conditioning and building walls.

Training and Human Resource Development

The quality of an organization's training and development program often determines the success with which it absorbs modern office technologies into its everyday operations. It is best to merge training in word processing with the overall personnel development program run by your corporate training department. This integration entails joint planning and scheduling between the office systems planners and the training unit. Thus the planners become ex officio members of the training unit, and some will eventually join the training unit as presenters of training programs. The training unit has responsibility for scheduling and other logistical matters.

Managers responsible for training may wish to read the IWP's (1979) booklet on *Human Resources and Word Processing*. This booklet, available from the IWP, reports the results of a survey to examine the interface between word processing technology and the people who make it work in business, industry, and government. The results show growing interest in the technology together with ambivalent feelings. Excerpts quoted from answers give insight into the potential fears of employees.

Among the many excellent training resources are the seminars and workshops presented by organizations such as the IWP (see Chapter 4) and the Society for Technical Communication (STC). The latter's annual convention features sessions for writers, graphic artists, and other communicators who need to learn how to use the new technology productively. For instance, Cuozzo (1981) gives a clear and interesting explanation of how computer graphics works and why writers need them.

Another excellent resource is Lake's (1981) article, "Think Training." Arguing that careful selection of a training program yields more efficient operations, better use of equipment, and higher productivity, Lake discusses the elements of a good training program and compares vendor-provided with in-house training programs.

Eventually, office support units will need to produce documentation for local procedures. Cecil's (1980) highly useful article on how to write your own manual includes sample formats and checklists. Readers who want more information can find it in Cecil's (1980) book, *Management of Word Processing Operations*.

Operator training. The goal of initial training is to teach operators how to use the word processor to accomplish most typing tasks. Initial training usually takes a day or two. It is needed when the equipment is installed and later when new operators are hired.

Advanced training follows initial training by three to six months, depending on an operator's familiarity with basic functions and features and on whether an operator's job requires advanced features. Some operators aren't capable of learning advanced features.

Firms that plan on outside training may want to read Helwig's (1981) article on Kelly Services, Inc.'s versatile, four-hour training course for WP operators. The course focuses on concepts, not specific systems, and was designed by Universal Training Systems Co. of Chicago. It is given in Kelly's branch offices. A second four-hour course, which takes place on the customer's premises and is free to the customer, helps the operator to become accustomed to the customer's system. Kelly hopes to train up to 50,000 operators in 1982.

Supervisor's training. Large firms will want special training for WP supervisors, lead operators, WP trainers, WP coordinators, and administrative assistants. Initially, a firm may want to use the services of outside trainers. Several organizations offer such training in the form of office automation seminars and workshops. Several articles listed in the bibliography (Henson & Sanders, 1980; Simmons, 1980; Wagoner, 1980) describe formal educational programs that train many operators and supervisors.

Managerial and staff training. Office automation enables workers to do old tasks in new ways. Managers and other originators of text need to learn the capabilities of the equipment so that they can make the best use of it and so that they know what to expect from the offices and staff.

With managers, staff, and executives, one useful resource is the IWP's (n.d.) *Command Dictation Manual,* available from the IWP, developed to give users of dictation equipment an acceptable and universally applicable set of specifications to cover all major dictating concerns. The instructions provide guidelines on organizing thoughts, specifying format, and the like. Unfortunately, this manual does not give instructions on how to handle the mechanics of the equipment.

Another useful resource is Spirt's (1981) article, which makes a persuasive case for training professionals on word processing equipment. Benefits cited include shorter time to produce ideas, greater insight into the creative uses of word processing, easier transfer to new equipment when that is necessary, and elimination of anxiety about using terminals.

Executive training. Modern office technologies work most efficiently when the senior officials in a firm understand and use the system. If your firm has executives who are not technologically oriented, start training with briefings and simple but typical services. Move gradually to more complex operations, always giving plenty of time for practice on activities an executive will perform daily. If your executives are technological zealots, give them a full course of training as rapidly as their schedule permits.

Measurement Standards

Help with the task of measurement standards can be found in a variety of articles. Hanson (1981) discusses flaws in current measurement techniques and recommends that manufacturers abandon concepts based on lines of type. Little (1980) provides a simple, effective way to measure typing output. He emphasizes the need to keep measurement to a useful minimum and to pay attention to the sources of error. Shafer (1981) argues that a well-coordinated performance measurement system reports all the facts needed to evaluate center operations. This excellent article gives step-by-step instructions for initiating such a system, including information requirements, data requirements, data gathering methods, and summarizing and reporting.

Applications

Applications support ensures the achievement of user objectives. Support for applications helps to achieve objectives more rapidly. Among the operations that benefit from support are managing the production of personalized form letters, setting up standard formats for frequent tasks, developing list processing systems, and defining storage schemes for quick retrieval of stored documents. More applications are discusssed in Chapter 9.

Hot Line

Immediate answers to questions give operators more productive work time and keep them from becoming afraid of the system. Questions may cover any day-to-day use of the system and its procedures. Some operators feel more comfortable when they can ask a person for help and don't have to rely on a manual. Some vendors of word processing products maintain a national hot line.

Coordination of User Groups

Local and/or in-house user groups enable staff to exchange ideas and develop professionally. Meetings and newsletters serve these groups well. In addition, some vendors sponsor user groups and newsletters (see Table 4.1, Chapter 4). Smaller organizations will probably want to enroll their staff in these groups as well as in professional organizations such as the International Information/ Word Processing Association. One probable result of such groups is reduced telephone calls to consultants as operators begin turning to one another for answers to questions.

Back-up Staff Support

Most organizations need to provide temporary replacements for ill or vacationing operators. One option is to temporarily relocate permanent staff. Another is to use office temporary services. Still another is Hedden's (1981) innovative concept—using a team of operators trained on many systems as floaters to fill in for ill or vacationing workers. Companies with more than one type of equipment will want to consult this article. Heddon reports that these floaters are frequently promoted to more responsible positions and that their training makes them prime candidates for becoming office systems analysts.

TECHNICAL SUPPORT

Technical support backs up customer support by providing technical hardware planning, problem tracking, and support for integrating both hardware and software.

Hardware Planning

Hardware planning, which occurs in the context of long-range planning, helps offices to make the best use of current investments without precluding improvements in the future. Hardware planning requires combined effort by a firm's purchasing and maintenance divisions, the vendors, office units, and the firm's long-range planners. Supporting efforts to prepare a site may include building or dividing rooms and installing electricity, coaxial cables, and air conditioning. Long-range planning reduces wasted expense by preventing duplicated effort.

Software Support

Software support maximizes system availability and allocates system resources fairly. Office technology, based partly on computer technology, includes software that requires maintenance just as the hardware does. Software doesn't break down as hardware does, but programs *do* need maintenance to correct flaws in logic and to add the ability to handle new tasks.

Software support also makes possible the linking of software on various pieces of equipment to do a task that can't be executed on any single piece of equipment. Software support also provides for management of the systems' storage resource, password security, and back-up and recovery facilities.

Hardware Integration

To prevent dilution of consultants' attention to impact on people and organizations, separate hardware integration service from other consulting functions. As Chapter 3 explains, integration and communication glue office systems together. As offices add electronic mail and message switching to word processing systems (or vice versa), hardware and software integration will become more complex and difficult.

For example, one organization wanted to merge address lists (stored on the data processing computer) with the text of form letters and print finished letters on a high-speed laser printer that normally served the computer system. A great deal of testing and cooperation between vendors went into this effort. Firms cannot always copy technical solutions from one another because the technologies haven't become standardized.

An even more extensive example is The Paperless Office (Brairton, 1981), which features the linked, communicating products of 22 vendors.

Breakdowns

All firms will want to centralize troubleshooting to prevent unnecessary expense, monitor vendors' performance, and spot equipment that needs to be replaced. Dedicate one telephone line for use by operators who think their equipment is broken. Have the contact person ask the appropriate diagnostic questions and direct testing to determine whether service is needed. (Some apparent equipment failure turns out to be operator error.) When service is needed, the contact person calls for it and works with the vendor until the equipment is back in service. He or she also records the problem for tracking and later statistical analysis to identify faulty equipment.

OFFICE SYSTEMS ROLES

The office systems support group should include at least five job roles: office systems consultant, customer service representative, application developer, software specialist, and project manager. Small firms will combine two or more of these roles in the same person. Large firms may have more than one person in one or more of these roles. Many firms will start with a small support unit and increase its size as the amount of equipment increases.

Qualifications. Consultants need technical experience in programming, analysis, telecommunications, and mini- and microcomputers. This background enables the consultant to help with hardware planning. Consultants must be able to work with people on all levels in the office. They need experience in human relations and organizational design to prepare them to design work areas, develop job specifications, chart systems flow, and market the office systems to be installed.

Duties and responsibilities. The consultant has the following duties and responsibilities:

- Assists with preinstallation planning—sociotechnical systems design.
- Acquires, develops, and maintains data collection tools and techniques.
- Provides technical information on office automation.
- Schedules and conducts demonstrations.
- Assesses needs, identifies objectives, and makes recommendations.
- Monitors use of installed equipment and helps to reassign underused equipment.
- Assists in teaching and training as needed.

Customer Support Representative

Qualifications. Teaching ability is a requirement, as is the ability to talk about office technologies without using jargon. Because this person cultivates and maintains contact with equipment operators, previous office and typing experience is very valuable.

Duties. The customer support representative's functions include training, answering the hot line, tracking problems, and starting and overseeing a user's group. Specifically, the customer support representative:

- Conducts overviews for new users before implementation.
- Schedules and conducts training.
- Prepares and reviews training modules.
- Gives guidance on technical problems to users of word processing.
- Coordinates user groups.
- Answers hot line questions.

Application Developer

Qualifications. Data processing experience, especially with mini- and microcomputers, is required.

Duties. In data processing, the parallel for the application developer is the analyst/programmer. The application developer has the following duties:

- Tests new equipment and evaluates prototype configurations.
- Assists users in developing data entry and records management systems.
- Writes programs for the equipment.
- Integrates office equipment and tests the linkages.

Software Specialist

Qualifications. The software specialist must have a detailed knowledge of the technologies involved as well as a data processing and communications background. Well-developed contacts with vendors are desirable.

Duties. The software specialist is much like the systems programmer in data processing. When storage loss occurs, the software specialist provides recovery. Specifically, the software specialist:

- Maintains retention/library procedures.
- Allocates document storage space.
- Maintains software.
- Loads new software to systems.
- Serves as liaison to vendors' software development staff.
- At the customer service representative's request, answers some users' questions about problems.

Project Manager

Requirements. The project manager must be able to incorporate new technologies into corporations. He or she must understand the technologies well enough to manage incorporation successfully and to know which technologies to avoid. He or she must also be able to work well with people at all levels.

Duties. The project manager:

- Coordinates and directs installation of equipment.
- Coordinates strategic planning for office automation.
- Plans, organizes, schedules, and controls the work activities of office systems personnel.
- Advises customers on the progress of projects.
- Develops recommendations of appropriate policies, procedures, and technical guidelines.
- Ensures compliance with company policies.

Enhancing Professionals'
Productivity
9 and Efficiency

Today much attention is focused on individual and organizational productivity, and, indeed, the development of information technologies holds great promise for increasing productivity. The dilemma is what aspect of technology to use to get the greatest shortrun gain. It is our contention that the development and spread of word processing throughout an organization will have the highest payoff in productivity.

In most organizations, modern office technology has been used first to automate secretarial work. Indeed, word processing, the first of the modern office technologies, has been the backbone application in most organizations, and successes and failures with it have been widely reported.

Executive tasks next captured the interest of systems developers. Today, a variety of executive support systems are used by some executives in many organizations. A few firms have even chosen executive support systems as their backbone technology. Unfortunately, many executives feel threatened by technology, resisting even the lowly dictating machine, which has been around for decades. As a result, we expect that full use of executive support systems won't occur until the turn of the twenty-first century, when a new generation of computer-literate executives has moved into positions of power.

Thus far, systems developers have largely overlooked a third group of potential users—the professionals and other staff members who, we feel, can make highly productive use of word processing in their work.

This chapter emphasizes the direct use of work stations by professionals including writers, public relations staff, lawyers, and others in business, industry, and academe. The focus is on document production, which is a major part of most professionals' job descriptions. Such use is already benefiting some firms and has the potential to benefit many more. Earlier chapters, especially Chapter 2, contain narratives that focus on other professional and managerial uses of work stations.

In 1979 very few professionals in business and industry were working directly with word or text processors. Most drafted by hand, dictation, or typewriter and handed the results to a typist or WP operator for keyboarding. The main reason for this situation was the vendor's and management's assumption that WP was a clerical tool, nothing more.

A few professionals who had managed to wangle terminals for themselves were learning how to insert photocomposition codes, but most were letting other departments handle that work. By May 1980, a show of hands in one session at a convention showed that nearly half the professionals present were working directly on a terminal, and many were learning the ropes of photocomposition.

Why? From the professionals' standpoint, the answer has to do with higher quality, faster production, greater creativity, less drudgery, and less chance of error. From the managers' and accountants' viewpoint, the answer has to do with dramatically lowered costs, higher productivity, value-added services, greater public visibility, and happier employees.

From one perspective, professionals' direct use of terminals should not surprise us. Journalists have been using them for years. Even when in the field, they no longer telephone in stories. They simply connect their portable terminals to telephones and transmit their stories. Furthermore, as management support systems have infiltrated "mahogany row," may executives have discovered that on certain documents, they would rather write on a terminal than dictate.

In this chapter, relying heavily on narratives, we argue for a broad view of electronic writing and communication that can benefit every professional in business, industry, and academe.

File Creation

Typing takes time. The fewer keystrokes needed to create a draft, the faster the draft will be done. The first professionals to work with WP terminals discovered three features that helped them draft more rapidly: document copying, format copying, and stored words and phrases.

The ability to *copy* paragraphs and formats from one document to another works in one of two ways, variously called "includ"ing, "supercopy"ing, and other terms. One form of this technique allows the professional, while working on one file, to look at another text file and copy passages from the stored file into the working file. Other systems make professionals take all or nothing of the second file (in which case they simply delete the parts they don't want).

Stored words and phrases also work in one of two ways. Both enable the professional to type the words once and assign a code to them. (The permitted length of the phrase varies from just a few characters to several pages.) After that, he or she types only the code. At that point, some word processors "read" the stored words and instantly write them on the screen. Others always show only the code on the screen. When the document prints, though, the processor "reads" what the code means and prints the stored words, not the code. For instance, we don't type "word processing system" anymore. Instead, we use /:wps/ in the text. When we print copy, the word processing program looks up the meaning of "wps" and inserts "word processing system."

Both features save a great many keystrokes and hold great power for the creative mind.

Jean Stephens, a middle-level manager, had just finished the final draft of a policy statement on word processing at Jones Manufacturing. She knew from her reading, the meeting, and conversations with other managers in many businesses that word processing policies were a hot topic. Chances were pretty good that the general principles in their statement would interest others. What's more, she reflected, publicity for the WP project would increase staff members' pride in the quality of work they were doing. So, after confirming the project with her supervisor and the chair of the word processing committee, she copied the policy file, added a few statistics from the company's data base, took out some of the topics that applied only to Jones Manufacturing, and submitted the resulting paper for consideration to the reviewers for a machine records conference. As she worked, her colleagues were able to review the working draft from their terminals, and when she had questions, she needed only to send an electronic message to the appropriate person. Often a response came back within an hour. The paper was accepted and presented, several months later, to an audience of 350. The document won a "Best Paper" award, and Jones got lots of publicity that cost only two workdays for writing, two travel days, and the expenses for the trip taken by the committee chairman, who presented the paper.

A few days later, also starting with the policy file and with her own professional interests in mind this time, Stephens started a paper for an upcoming convention of technical writers, many of whom would be involved in word processing policy development just as she had been. This time she improvised a dialogue to introduce the topic and focused on the special needs of technical writers. As she worked, she consulted with the firm's technical writers to ascertain that she was reflecting their needs accurately. That paper was also accepted. Again, the cost was low—about two writing days, three travel/convention days, and travel costs. For Jones, the payback was publicity and job applications from several listeners who thought Jones sounded like an exciting place to work. For Stephens, the payoffs were a line on her résumé and a pay raise the following year.

As work progressed through a technical study, Stephens copied parts of the first paper and parts of several instructional documents to draft a paper on the social and technical factors that word processing planners must consider. This paper went to a special interest group of an association of computing professionals. Later, with a few more changes, Stephens converted the paper into an article for a technical journal.

A bit later, she and the person who chaired the word processing planning committee drafted a paper to submit to an annual contest for papers on management information systems (MIS). This time she started the document with paragraphs from the final planning document as well as from the policy statement. The focus was on the information management aspects of word processing.

In addition, meantime, Stephens took advantage of her files to write regular short articles for the company newsletter, keeping all staff informed of progress on the planning for office automation. She also translated the policy document and several instructional documents into a Jones Manufacturing word processing handbook. Throughout the process, colleagues and supervisors kept in touch with her work through their own terminals. When the handbook was done, she used the scheduling module to set up a meeting of those who needed to discuss the document.

Revision of Text

Naturally, the rough drafts created this way need lots of editing. Each of Stephens' documents, targeted for a different audience, required a lead sentence or paragraph tailored to the readers' interests. Each one required different data. Some required graphics, prepared on the graphics module. Juxtaposing paragraphs from different documents requires changing transitions. But editing is, to quote one vendor, "No Problem." Best of all, when Stephens finishes her work, she has clean copy minutes later, and colleagues and supervisors can check her work from their own work stations. In her view, the reworking is rather like working with clay: the same shapeless gray, uninspired lump can become any one of a variety of interesting pieces of art with its own unique combination of shape and color.

John Wright, a specialist in technical manuals, always started documents with a file of notes and musings on the topic, using it much as he used to use a scratch pad. From those musings he'd build an outline, taking advantage of the automatic number counter so he could move parts of the outline around without having to renumber everything. Gradually he'd build from a topic outline to a sentence outline, filled in at lower levels.

When he was ready to start the document, he copied sentences from the outline and used the same stored words and phrases. He copied format requirements from other documents, including the space for illustrations. As soon as he had a draft, he'd send a message to the project programmer, who would look at the file, offer comments, and possibly insert some of his own examples. One handy feature of the system was the ability to write notes in a file that would appear on the screen with the text but not print unless he specifically asked for them. Often, he and the programmer would consult several times, occasionally experimenting with layout until both were satisfied with the document as a whole. Most of these exchanges were completed in a day or less.

Revising and updating old documents was even easier because the files already existed. In the time since the previous publication, he and the programmer would have been keeping an electronic file of notes about topics to be added, corrections to be made, layouts that didn't seem to be working, sections on which the programmer had received calls for clarification, and so forth. Some programmers would already have roughed out a file of updates; others simply sent over typed or handwritten pages. Wright would look at the document as a whole, finding the place to make each insert, change, and deletion.

Whether he was drafting or updating, Wright appreciated having his own terminal. He could try out an idea in half the time it used to take him to write instructions for a word processing operator. If he didn't like an idea, he could change it easily, again in less time than instructing an operator would have taken. He also knew that having his own terminal let him work much faster. His daily records showed that he was handling between three and five times as much material as under the old system. Weekly differences were mainly due to differences in the amount of revision versus creation of new text: the more revision, the greater the productivity.

Furthermore, the company's shared system made it easy for him to communicate with other professionals, thus speeding the completion of documents. Managers could supervise from their own terminals and frequently sent messages to him. Lawyers in the legal department could check legal implications while the document was still in draft form. Graphics specialists could check and correct his illustrations, and programmers could add data and examples from their own files. When the final document was ready, it could be transmitted directly to the photocomposer.

Like Stephens, Wright appreciates the ease of revision. Both Stephens and Wright appreciate the advanced features that automatically number outlines and create tables of contents, lists of tables and illustrations, and indexes. Before automation, the work was repetitive and boring, always done at the last minute under pressure and always at risk of copying errors. Now they can have contents and lists throughout the process, and their existence sometimes shows errors in topic level or order. Sometimes the length of sections as reflected in page numbers shows that an unimportant topic has been treated in too much depth, or an important one in too little depth. When a document is too long, the table of contents can help professionals decide which parts to cut first.

The basic process is simple. Writers use a special code to mark the chapter titles and headings to be used in the tables and lists. These don't print when the text prints, but when the writer asks the system to print the table of contents, it reads the codes, lists the marked items, and adds the page numbers on which they appear!

Similarly, indexing programs let writers insert nonprinting notes in the text as they write. These notes tell the index program the exact words to put in the index and the level of the entry. Running the index program lists the entries and types the page numbers on which they occur. If a later revision changes the page numbers, the writers simply run a new index.

For Stephens and Wright the important point is that the automation of hack work and the ease of communication have freed them to use their creative powers to their fullest. Their fellow staff member Kim White agrees.

Kim White, a professional in the public relations department, was preparing a recruiting brochure for Jones Manufacturing. She had drafted the text and was now experimenting with various layouts of pictures. Her terminal's split-screen capability really helped with this task, enabling her to show and compare two different layouts at once. When she had made her choice, she put in photocomposition codes to specify type style and sizes and then transmitted the copy to a photocomposer for a trial printing.

Next, White copied the brochure text and used it as the basis for an article on recruiting for the May issue of the company magazine. Later she would use two paragraphs from the article in the company's annual report, and several paragraphs would be used to start a news release on Jones's approach to the recruiting season. In both the article and the annual report, she used statistics from the company data base and a graphics module to prepare illustrations. Help with both these tasks was only as far away as an electronic message to a friendly programmer.

White appreciates the experimental possibilities of the split-screen terminal and the ability to "set type" on her own work. Knowing her material and her audiences as well as she does, she has a knack for putting text, layout, and typefaces together in an attractive package.

Benefits for All

Professionals and managers feel less stress because they don't have to worry about errors creeping into a document that someone else is handling. A revision can now be accomplished in hours, sometimes minutes, from starting to work to putting a final copy in an envelope. On proposals and project reports with firm deadlines and short time lines, the automation often makes unnecessary a crash effort that exhausts the time and patience of everyone in the vicinity.

HOW MUCH DOES THIS COST?

Firman (1980, p. C-129) found that the cost of equipment, whether purchased or leased, was much lower than the cost of the employees the equipment replaced. At Firman Publications, a producer of technical documents, the equipment replaced between seven and ten staff members (depending on how Firman calculated). Additional costs—floor space, special desks, and supplies—exist but hardly make a dent in the savings.

In 1980, Firman (1981) did a study to compare the cost of traditional versus WP-based publication operations. The bottom line for traditional methods came to $239 per page; for his WP-based operation, the cost was $135 per page. When Firman reported his findings to the firms surveyed, several responded with surprise that the traditional figure was as low as $235 per page! They had thought their costs were higher!

WHAT ARE THE BENEFITS?

We've alluded to some benefits, such as greater visibility for both firms and professionals and greater job satisfaction for professionals. We've been quite specific about the benefit in lower costs. Other benefits include:

- *Timeliness:* brochures and manuals reach the market at the time a product does; articles get published while a topic still interests the public.
- *Usability:* a well-tested, well-designed document will satisfy users. They won't have to pick up the phone to get questions answered.
- *Accuracy:* testing, checking, and WP-controlled editing ensure a higher degree of accuracy than is true with typing. Furthermore, because drafts look much like the final copy, minor errors are more likely to be caught in review.
- *Thoroughness:* standard formats such as text mapping (a documentation technique), which force a response to specific topics, ensure that all crucial topics are considered.

HOW DO I GET OUR PROFESSIONALS STARTED?

Start by letting your professionals participate in the choice of a system. As the dialogue at the beginning suggests, professionals demand more of a word processor than most clerical staff do. You don't want to choose a system that might suit your secretaries but is too slow and limited to suit your professionals.

Your first installation will probably serve bread-and-butter secretarial applications because that is where your most pressing needs probably exist. However, include professionals' use of word processors in your long-range plans. As soon as possible, order terminals for all professionals who want one (our assumption is that any firm large enough to employ staff writers and other professionals is large enough to be choosing some form of shared system). If the initial cost of terminals is prohibitive, consider getting OCR equipment so that drafts can be typed on a typewriter, releasing the word processing terminals for revising. Don't force the few resisters. Many will come around when the benefits become apparent.

WHO OWNS THE WRITTEN WORK?

Unless company policy prohibits, let professionals hold their own copyrights as authors or coauthors. Whatever the policy, make sure everyone knows what it is. Some firms require all employees to sign a statement that transfers to the employer ownership and earnings from *any* writing done by the employee. Some let the employee keep authorship but require them to turn over any earnings. Some make these demands only for work done on company time. Work done at other times belongs to the employee. With professional articles and conference papers, there is rarely any problem. When money is involved, though, make a firm policy and make certain the professionals know it.

ARE THERE ANY PROBLEMS MANAGERS SHOULD KNOW ABOUT?

The only real problems experienced so far have come from the blurring of job specifications as defined by technology. Some managers have persisted in classifying as secretaries anyone who uses a terminal. Professionals, naturally, object. As more and more managers get their own terminals, that problem should fade away. A tougher problem has been union objections to having professionals set photocomposition codes—a thorny problem because some professionals know better than compositors how they want the text to look. Furthermore, it saves time to have the professional set type along with other steps.

Overall, the weight of evidence, as with office automation in general, favors the innovative spirit that is putting terminals on professionals' desks.

WHAT ARE THE IMPLICATIONS?

As studies of executive support systems have shown, modern technology changes the way we think and work. Professionals with terminals are showing that technology can also change the way we create and use documents—speeding up drafting, enabling higher quality revision, and permitting creative file sharing.

Thus far, Firman Publications and other firms have found that desktop terminals are a good investment for technical writers (producers of documentation, instructions, proposals, speeches, articles, etc.). They can also be a good investment for members of a public relations staff (producers of brochures, annual reports, company newsletters and magazines, news releases, etc.), advertising and sales staffers (producers of advertisements, advertising flyers, etc.), legal counselors, and other professionals who have to turn out attractive, well-written, well-formatted documents and who need, therefore, the ability to experiment freely with format and design as they relate to substance.

Some offices, of course, would be served adequately by a few shared terminals because most of the employees don't have a full day's worth of writing to do each day. Regardless of the number of terminals in an office, the important points for managers are:

- Professionals who write can often do it better on a terminal, which allows experimentation with layout and organization.
- It often takes professionals less time to do the work themselves than to transmit instructions to an operator.
- Electronic writing speeds up and improves the quality of thinking.
- Supervision and review can occur on work stations.

Eventually, we expect to see multipurpose terminals in nearly every room of most businesses and industries, easily available to any staff member who needs to check data, send a memo, or draft a letter or report. Even workers on assembly lines will someday be able to step up to a terminal and whip off a suggestion to the company's electronic suggestion box.

At the end of the nineteenth century, technological zealots squabbled with technoresisters over the relative merits of the horse and buggy versus the automobile. Today, we have an analogous situation. Technology separates many in the same firm as technological zealots and technoresisters debate the merits of the automated office. Tomorrow, though, with terminals in every office and on many desks, technology may well bring us closer together in an electronic version of the quality circles that have worked so well in Japan.

Bibliography

Advanced communications option offers high transmission speeds via TWX network. 1980 *Administrative Management* XLI (10, October):63.

This article reviews telex communications on QYX and Wang products.

BAKER, W. H. 1980. Are schools doing their job? *Words* 9 (3, October-November):19-21.

After a study of 105 schools, Baker concludes that WP instruction is offered in many post-secondary institutions throughout the country. Only 25% of the WP instructors have had actual business experience involving the use of WP equipment. Nearly all educators have attended WP seminars to help them prepare to teach in the WP area. Most schools have non-CRT equipment. Demand is greatest for training in operation; significantly fewer students want to become WP systems analysts. Finally, only about 25% of the schools anticipate no major changes in the WP offerings in the near future.

BARBER, RICHARD D. 1980. Stretch your word processing potential—Parts I and II. *Words* 8 (6, April-May):29-32 and 9 (1, June-July):22-30.

In Part I Barber explains how OCR captures information to eliminate costly bottlenecks in production. In Part II he tells how advanced OCR refinements and applications will soon augment sales of word processing equipment.

BAXTER, R. I. and WILK, E. S. 1981. Primary considerations for integrating systems. *Words* 9 (4, December-January):20-24.

Baxter and Wilk discuss the complexities and basic practicality of integrated systems. The benefits include efficient use of available resources, reduction of paper and files, cost-effective systems management, common procedures, and enhanced communications.

BEISWINGER, G. L. 1981. The electronic freelancer. *Writer's Digest* (April):26-27.

This article, on the uses of word processors to free-lance writers, would be useful mainly to technical and business writers and editors who are using word processors instead of typewriters.

BENTLEY, E. 1981. Techno-Resistance. *Savvy* (February):40-43.

Bentley describes many of the fears staff members have about the new office technology. She offers suggestions and makes some predictions. One major suggestion: get broad participation from the beginning.

BIERMAN, P. 1981. Memories are made of this. *Personal Computing* (June):41-49.

Like Hughes (see below), Bierman describes the nature and types of memory in computers. Unlike Hughes, Bierman gives little historical background.

BLACKMARR, B. R. 1981. Information management comes of age. *Words* 10 (1, June-July):18-22.

This article gives practical guidance to WP professionals who need to learn information management skills.

1980. Blending word processing and telex. *Modern Office Procedures* 25 (10, October):196-199.

This article tells how Agfa-Gevaert, a world-wide marketer of photographic products, integrated telex communications and word processing to solve problems in communication between U.S. and European offices.

BOSTROM, R. P. 1980. A socio-technical perspective on MIS Implementation. Paper presented at ORSA/TIMS National Conference, Colorado Springs, Colorado (November).

Bostrom discusses the social aspects of technical change in organizations.

BOYD, A., GOOD, P., And VEIT, S. 1981. A user's guide to operating systems. *Personal Computing* (May):27-32, 87, 108.

Operating systems are a computer's housekeepers. Boyd and his associates explain the details and provide summary charts.

BRAIRTON, C. V. 1981. The paperless office. *Working Woman* 6 (7, July):42-43.

Brairton describes Micronet Inc.'s paperless office, which is located in Washington, D.C.'s Watergate Mall complex. Already visited by nearly 8,000 people, including top managers from firms such as 3M and American Telephone and Telegraph, the office has integrated products from 22 manufacturers. The seven full-time staffers and affiliated consultants sit at modular work stations equipped with a desk-top terminal, microfiche reader, and telephone. Brairton reports that some staff have learned the system in as little as half a day. Breaking old habits takes longer—it took one new staff person three months to break the habit of keeping paper files.

BRILES, S. M. 1981. Interequipment communication. *Technical Communication* 28 (3):4-7, 62-63.

Briles's excellent article explains clearly, with illustrations, the terms and techniques needed to understand communication between word processors, photocomposers, computers, and so forth.

BURSKY, D. 1981. Disk memories: What you should know before you buy them. *Personal Computing* (April):20-27.

Bursky provides an overview of the disk memory market, with detailed information on how to choose the best type of disk drive for given applications. He covers both hard and floppy disks, describing the pro's and con's of each.

CASSIN, J. 1981. The use of micrographics in achieving productivity. *The Office* 93 (1, January):114.

This article explains the uses of micrographics.

CECIL, P. B. 1980. Write your own word processing manual. *Modern Office Procedures* 25 (2, February):135-140.

This highly useful article tells how to write your own manual and includes sample formats and checklists. The article is taken from the author's book, *Management of Word Processing Operations* (Menlo Park, California: Benjamin/Cummings Publishing Co., 1980).

COHEN, J. A. 1980. *How to computerize your small business.* Englewood Cliffs, N.J.: Prentice-Hall.

Cohen gives clear, detailed, step-by-step guidance on how to computerize a small business. The book would be especially useful to managers of small businesses who planned to use the same computer for both word and data processing.

CUOZZO, J. A., JR. 1981. Three-dimensional interactive graphics systems: Revolutionizing technical illustrations production in the 1980s. *Proceedings, 28th International Technical Communication Conference.* Pittsburgh: Society for Technical Communication 6-8 to 6-12.

Cuozzo gives a clear and interesting explanation of how computer graphics works and why writers need them.

Datapro Research Corporation. 1978. Function and form in the automated office. *The Current Office.* Report #A10-100. Delran, N.J.: Datapro Research Corporation:102-105.

This report reduces the parts of the modern office to the functional simplicity of "a one-pencil, one-pad, one-drawer office operation," summarized in the acronym IPSOD—input, processing, storage, output, and distribution.

DAUBITZ, P. C. 1981. What do consultants do? And why are they hired? *The Office* 93 (5, May):170-171, 174.

Daubitz explains what consultants do and how to evaluate consulting firms.

1980. Delivering the electronic mail at Johns-Manville. *Modern Office Procedures* 25 (2, February):120-124.

This article explains in detail one firm's use of electronic mail and word processing to speed up operations.

n.d. *Designing technical manuals.* Pembroke, Mass.: Firman Publications.

This excellent booklet tells how Firman Publications, which creates and produces technical manuals, uses word processing to prepare a high-quality, profitable product.

1981. Dictation and electronic typing step up efficiency at FAA facility in Atlanta. *The Office* 93 (2, February):19, 65.

This article reports dramatic savings after installing dictation and word processing equipment. All equipment is compatible, and first-year productivity rose between 30 and 40%.

Educator's Advisory Council. n.d. *The reference guide to word processing education.* Willow Grove, Pennsylvania: IWP.

This document lists and describes word processing education programs across the United States.

1981. Evaluation of shared word processing systems. Unpublished report. Bloomington, Indiana: Office of Information and Computer Services, Indiana University.

This document is an internal report of Indiana University.

FARMER, B. E. 1981. W. Bell and Company puts typesetting and WP on speaking terms. *Words* 9 (5, February-March):38-42.

Farmer describes how one firm got its word processor to communicate with a typesetter.

FEIDELMAN, L. 1981. A top-down approach to better office systems. *The Office* 93 (1, January):97-98.

Feidelman reviews the benefits of providing all executive personnel with terminals for calendar-keeping, scheduling, tickler reminding, and other functions. He concludes that when organizations use this "top-down" approach, executives can spend more time doing what they are paid to do.

FIELDEN, R. n.d. *Writing a word processing grant proposal.* Willow Grove, Pennsylvania: International Word Processing Association.

This booklet, useful mainly to educational institutions, tells how to write a grant proposal to get word processing equipment for educational purposes. Useful features are a resource list of grant and funding agencies, sample proposal and budget, and a list of schools that offer WP courses and curricula.

1980. Film file facilitates finding fiche. *Modern Office Procedures* 25 (2, February):68-72.

This article describes one firm's use of microfiche to prevent misplaced records, keep them clean, and make records easier to find. In addition, the system has reduced costs by up to 75%.

FIRMAN, A. H. 1980. Managing a professional level WP system. *Proceedings, 27th International Technical Communication Conference.* Minneapolis: Society for Technical Communication.

Firman, a pioneer at putting word processors directly in writers' hands, tells how and why he advocates this approach.

_____. 1981. WP as a tool in improving the cost-effectiveness of technical publications. *Proceedings, 28th International Technical Communication Conference.* Pittsburgh: Society for Technical Communication.

Firman, following up his 1980 paper, provides hard statistics to support his assertion that WP for writers is profitable.

FLORES, I. 1981. An introduction to word processing. *Technical Communication* 28 (1):12-16.

This article explains word processing to technical communicators.

GOLDFIELD, R. J. 1980a. The automated office in the 1980s. *Dun's Review* (March):129-150.

Goldfield, a specialist in office automation, discusses the reasons for office automation, the key planning issues, the importance of top management support, speed of implementation, risks and costs, systems architecture, and management of the people involved.

_____. 1980b. Records automation. *Administrative Management* XLI (10, October):82.

Goldfield shows how to build a convincing case for records automation.

HANSON, W. B. 1981. Measured standards for word processing. *The Office* 93 (5, May):166, 168.

Hanson discusses flaws in current measurement techniques and recommends that manufacturers abandon concepts based on lines of type.

HEDDEN, B. G. 1981. Mobile operator concept in corporate word processing. *The Office* 93 (2, February):108, 112.

Heddon describes an innovative concept—using a team of operators trained on many systems as floaters to fill in for ill or vacationing workers. Companies with more than one type of equipment will want to consult this article. Heddon reports that these floaters are frequently promoted to more responsible positions and that their training makes them prime candidates for becoming office systems analysts.

HELWIG, T. 1981. Harnessing auxiliary power for office automation. *Words* 9 (5, February-March):17-20.

Helwig points out problems in the word processing industry—too many products, overloaded educational programs, inadequate management, and ineffective use of resources. He discusses ways to deal with these problems and cautions to consider when dealing with consultants, personnel placement bureaus, training, and service bureaus.

HENSON, L. and SANDERS, M. 1980. Schools practice professionalism in the WP classroom. *Words* 9 (3, October-November):26-28.

Henson and Sanders describe WP training at Jefferson College, a two-year school in Hillsboro, Missouri, that awards a one-year certificate and a two-year degree. At the beginning of the second semester, the WP lab becomes a WP center in which students rotate through the positions of supervisor, assistant supervisor, correspondence specialist, editor (and proofreader), records manager, and administrative specialist. This program helps students to learn procedures, develop professionalism, and progress from being students to being professionals.

HUGHES, E. M. 1981. A beginner's guide to memory. *onComputing* 3 (1):18-26.

In an article directed toward microcomputer users, Hughes explains clearly the origins and technical implications of various kinds of computer memory.

HUGHES, J. G., JR. 1980. Guidelines for selecting a text-editing machine. *Word Processing Systems* 7 (10, October):65.

Hughes tells us how to choose word processing equipment. He emphasizes fit to a company's applications, integration into existing office operations, and reliable vendor support.

ILSON, R. 1980. Recent research in text processing. *Words* 9 (1, June-July):33-34, 52-54.

144

Ilson tells of software being designed specifically to uncomplicate format requirements in document processing.

1981. Innovative training program introduced for word processors. *The Office* 93 (3, March):66, 170.

This article describes Kelley Services, Inc.'s versatile, four-hour training course for WP operators. The course focuses on concepts, not specific systems, and was designed by Universal Training Systems Co. of Chicago. It is given in Kelly's branch offices. A second four-hour course, which takes place on the customer's premises and is free to the customer, helps the operator to become accustomed to the customer's system. Kelley hopes to train up to 50,000 operators in 1982.

1980. Intelligent copying is growing up. *Modern Office Procedures* 25 (2, February):58-60.

This article defines, explains, and lists the advantages of using intelligent copier/printers.

International Word Processing Association. 1979. *Human resources and word processing.* Willow Grove, Pennsylvania: International Word Processing Association.

This booklet, available from II/WP, reports the results of a survey to examine the interface between the new word processing technology and the people who make it work in business, industry, and government. The results show growing interest in the technology together with ambivalent feelings. Excerpts quoted from answers give insight into the potential fears of employees.

_____. n.d. *Command dictation manual.* Willow Grove, Pennsylvania: IWP.

This manual, available from IWP, was developed to give users of dictation equipment an acceptable and universally applicable set of specifications to cover all major dictating concerns. The instructions cover guidelines such as organizing thoughts, specifying format, and the like. This is not a manual on how to handle the mechanics of the equipment.

_____. n.d. *IWP word processing industry directory.* Willow Grove, Pennsylvania: IWP.

This directory is a resource list of products, services, publications, and schools.

_____. n.d. *IWP word processing glossary.* Willow Grove, Pennsylvania: IWP.

This glossary, a reference work of terms important in word processing and dictation, also includes some communication and computer terms.

145

Bibliography

JENNINGS, W. R. 1980. The importance of text processing in a technical environment. *The Office* 91 (2, February):18-20.

This article describes the use of integrated word processing and photocomposition equipment in an Idaho engineering laboratory.

KAPLAN, H. M. 1980. Voice processing speeds communication to step up productivity. *Words* 9 (1, June–July):40-43.

Kaplan explains technological developments in digital voice recording that will offer a variety of ways to make executives more productive.

LAKE, B. 1981. Think training. *Words* 9 (5, February-March):21-25.

Lakes argues that careful selection of a training program yields more efficient operations, better use of equipment, and higher productivity. He discusses the elements of a good training program and compares vendor-provided with in-house training programs.

LIBERMAN, M. 1980. Pushing buttons to improve writing skills? *Words* 8 (6, April-May):14-15.

Liberman, an expert on computer-assisted instruction (CAI), speculates on possible adaptations of WP to teaching writing.

LITTLE, J. R. 1980. Measured typing output: Does it help or hinder? *The Office* 91 (2, February):24-32.

Little provides a simple, effective way to measure typing output. He emphasizes the need to keep measurement to a useful minimum and to pay attention to the sources of error.

LODAHL, T. M. 1980. Cost-benefit concepts and applications for office automation. *Proceedings of AFIPS 1980 Office Automation Conference. March (Atlanta):171-175.*

This paper describes cost-displacement in light of the value of a professional's time.

McCABE, H. M. and POPHAM, E. 1977. *Word Processing.* New York: Harcourt, Brace Jovanovich.

This slim paperback describes the emergence of the word processing profession and pays careful attention to job ladders and job descriptions. It also contains several excellent case studies.

MAKOWER, J. 1980. Information systems. *Mainliner* (October):133-144.

Makower's well-written article reports on six office technologies, choices of equipment, changes in the office environment, and upcoming automation conferences.

_____. 1981. Computers '81: Planning your next system. *Eastern Review* (May):93-104.

Makower summarizes steps in planning for computers and discusses several case histories.

MARCUS, J. E. 1980. New office technologies: Cost analysis. Stanford, California: Stanford University.

This paper discusses in depth the concepts of cost-displacement and value-added work.

MARSHALL, E. 1981. FDA sees no radiation risk in VDT screens. *Science* 212 (5 June):1120-1121.

Marshall, reviewing research on and complaints about the radiation hazards possibly associated with using VDT screens, finds that "eye strain may be a problem, but federal officials are unpersuaded by x-ray and microwave complaints."

MEYERS, E. D., JR. 1981. Systems unite. *Words* 10 (1, June-July):40-44.

Meyers, director of the Research Computing Division of Boys Town Center for the Study of Youth Development, explains how he combined both DP and WP functions to produce the codebook for a research project. Meyers explains the procedure step by step and gives several illustrations.

1981. Micrographic technology allows bank to retrieve heavy volume of records. *The Office* 93 (5, May): 172, 176.

This article explains how a bank has used micrographic technology to eliminate backlog and speed up retrieval of records.

1981. Monsanto's unusual approach in creating an automated system. *The Office* 9C (2, February):79-80.

This article describes Monsanto's installation of an automated office system that serves professionals and secretaries.

MULLINS, C. J. 1980a. *The complete writing guide to preparing reports, proposals, memos, etc.* Englewood Cliffs, N.J.: Prentice-Hall.

This book describes a systematic approach to writing that integrates writing with word processing from the notes-and-outline stage through checking of the final document.

_____. 1980b. The computer as nitpicking copy editor. *Proceedings, 27th International Technical Communication Conference.* Minneapolis: Society for Technical Communication.

This paper describes word processing techniques that help writers to correct and proofread documents.

MULLINS, C. J. and WEST, T. W. 1981. Word processing and office technology: Policies and plans. Paper presented at CUMREC '81 and published in the *Proceedings.* Miami: CUMREC.

This paper summarizes the policies and plans for word processing at Indiana University.

147

————. 1981. Word processing for technical writers and teachers. *Proceedings, 28th International Technical Communication Conference.* Pittsburgh: Society for Technical Communication.

This paper summarizes Indiana University's policies and plans for word processing with special attention to the needs of teachers and writers.

————. 1981. Word processing and office technology: A path to the future. *CAUSE/EFFECT* (September):18-23.

This paper emphasizes the need for word processing planners to keep both technical and social concerns in mind.

NIEDERRITER, D. 1981. Information management resource guide. *Words* 10 (1, June-July):23-26.

Niederriter provides a list of resources for professionals who are learning about information management.

1981. OCR page reader helps firm decentralize word processing. *The Office* 93 (2, February):88.

This article tells how Allied Chemical Corporation uses an OCR page reader to put into a word processor pages typed on ordinary selectric typewriters.

ODIORNE, G. S. 1981. *The change resisters.* Englewood Cliffs, N.J.: Prentice-Hall.

Odiorne discusses the general resistance to change, of which resistance to modern office technology is a part, and suggests ways to deal with resisters.

1975. The office of the future. *Business Week* (June 30):48-49.

This article is one of the earliest on the office of the future.

1980. Open plan complements a conventional space. *Modern Office Procedures* 25 (10, October):136-137.

This article explains how to use colorful, inexpensive dividers to give privacy to individual work stations.

PANTAGES, A. 1980. Office automation. *Working Woman* (November): 11-28.

Pantages explores all facets of office automation. She provides a very useful glossary of technical terms and short interview-reports on the views of word processing specialists such as Amy D. Wohl.

PENN, I. A. 1981. A friendly letter to vendors of word processing equipment. *The Office* 93 (2, February):57-60, 123.

Penn points out some of the hard-sell vendor tactics that managers need to beware of.

PERRY, R. 1981. A writer's guide to word processors. *Writer's Digest* (April):21-30.

This article, on the uses of word processors to free-lance writers, would be useful mainly to technical and business writers and editors who are using word processors instead of typewriters.

PRINCE, J. S. 1980. Environments that work for people. *Administrative Management* XLI (10, October):36-41, 65.

This well-illustrated article goes into great detail on environmental factors that help to keep workers comfortable on the job.

REDMOND, P. A., JR. 1981. Mustering the right conversion method takes knowledge—and sometimes a little wizardry. *Words* 10 (1, June-July):30-32.

Redmond explains in simple language the meaning of and techniques for converting words and data from one system to another. He also discusses the need for comparing the costs of different conversion methods.

RIDER, M. E. 1981. Merging the best of word and data processing for purchasing in Virginia. *The Office* 93 (2, February):22, 27.

Rider reports a case study of one organization's movement into combined word and data processing.

RINGLE, L. E. 1981. The electronic interview. *Words* 10 (October-November):20-23.

Ringle describes an ingenious system for having the word processing equipment interview job candidates.

RIVERS, D. A. 1980. Programmable communications help make the connections. *Word Processing Systems* 7 (10, October):35, 67.

Rivers points out that programmable communications enable operators to change communication parameters. Important features to check out are protocol, mode, character length, baud rate, code set, parity, end-of-line character, duplex, and column width. Rivers defines terms and tells what to look for.

ROSEN, A. and FIELDEN, R. 1977. *Word processing*. Englewood Cliffs, N.J.: Prentice-Hall.

One of the major text books on word processing.

SCANNELL, T. 1980a. Focus on people urged for office automation. *Computerworld* (September 22):16.

Scannell discusses management's attitude toward the "unfeeling black box" and suggests ways to deal with that attitude.

_____. 1980b. Managers found resisting office automation. *Computerworld* (September 22):15.

Scannell discusses management's avoidance of automation and wasted time. Many of his statistics come from Goldfield's (1980a) report discussed earlier.

SCHUMANN, A. 1981. How to develop a useful work station analysis. *The Office* 93 (3, March):122, 154-158.

Schumann describes the development of a useful work station from beginning (a job description) to end. He recommends developing a mental image of the job, thinking in abstract terms rather than searching through catalogs. Catalogs are useful only after the designer has a clear, firm picture of the work station sketched out. He recommends the use of carpets and plants to give workers a sense of being in a luxurious environment.

SCHWARTZ, B. 1981. The video display terminal controversy: Smoke or fire. *Words* 10 (1, June-July):34-38.

Schwartz discusses the various grievances that have been launched against the VDT. Taken point by point, the concerns aren't valid. Schwartz gives good advice on ways to avoid problems.

SHAFER, J. C. I. 1981. Clinching management decisions. *Words* 9 (6, April-May):30-34.

Shafer argues that a well-coordinated performance measurement system reports all the facts needed to evaluate center operations. She gives step-by-step instructions for initiating such a system including information requirements, data requirements, data gathering methods, and summarizing and reporting.

SIMMONS, B. R. 1980. Phoenix Community College implements a model WP program to train students and serve administrators. *Words* 9 (3, October-November):31-34.

Simmons describes the course of WP instruction at Phoenix Community College. This program was Arizona's first and has since been copied by six other community colleges in the area. The program's WP center has gradually become a service bureau for the campus.

SMITH, P. S. 1980. Making woopie: A professional writer learns WP. *Proceedings, 27th International Technical Communication Conference.* Minneapolis: Society for Technical Communication.

Smith describes the demise of her technical-writing firm, based on typewriters and secretaries, and her subsequent success with Firman Technical Publications, Inc., a WP-based firm.

————. 1981. Creating cost-effective publications with the aid of WP. *Proceedings, 28th International Technical Communication Conference.* Pittsburgh: Society for Technical Communication.

Smith argues that the integration of WP into the creation/production process gives professional communicators complete control over the format of a publication as well as its content. This control allows rearrangement and experimentation without a major cost penalty.

SOLOMON, A. H. 1980. The merging of telecommunications and information processing: The technological underpinnings. *Computerworld* (January 21):1-17.

This excellent article, a *Computerworld* "in depth" report, gives background on the technologies of telecommunications and information processing and explains how the two fit together, what applications they can be applied to, and what the future might hold.

1981. Speech peripherals make computers more human. *Personal Computing* (June):19-20, 35-38, 86-87.

This article reviews the state of the art in voice processing. It includes a guide to vendors.

SPIRT, D. 1981. Professionals should know how to operate word processing equipment. *The Office* 93 (2, February):36, 41.

Spirt makes a persuasive case for training professionals on word processing equipment. Benefits include shorter time to produce ideas, greater insight into the creative uses of word processing, easier transfer to new equipment when that is necessary, and loss of anxiety about using terminals.

STEINBRECHER, D. 1980. When time is the only consideration, then the only way is RUSH. *Word Processing Systems* 7 (10, October):17-18.

This article tells how one firm handles document priority in a high-pressure organization.

STULTZ, R. 1982. *The word processing handbook.* Englewood Cliffs, N.J.: Prentice-Hall.

Stultz gives very good and detailed advice on choice of word processing equipment. He includes detailed definitions of technical terms.

TIFFANY, S. 1979. A word processing shopper's survival kit. *Administrative Management* (October).

Tiffany has lots of good advice for shoppers. It is summarized in Chapter 6.

TUNISON, E. F. 1981. The word processing generation. *Working Woman* (June):60-63.

Tunison describes WP systems and operations in three different sites: The White House, PepsiCo, and Johns-Manville.

VEKTERIS, T. and KENNY, A. A. 1981. WP service bureaus balance center capabilities and user needs. *Words* 9 (5, February-March): 26-28, 54.

This article lists and describes several WP service bureaus.

WAGONER, K. P. 1980. Emerging trends in WP education. *Words* 9 (3, October-November):22-25.

Wagoner draws several conclusions from a study of 176 schools. Among these are: (1) Some four-year institutions emphasize operations; others, the integrative aspects of WP and office information systems. Two popular courses are Word Processing Concepts and Word Processing Management. (2) Many schools are introducing courses to improve basic English skills. (3) Most WP programs have a variety of equipment. (4) Some schools are beginning to teach file maintenance and retrieval skills.

WALSHE, W. A. 1980. Word processing. *Administrative Management* XLI (10, October):80.

Walshe, discussing word processing on small business computers, offers several cautions and lists minimum requirements for software.

WATERHOUSE, S. A. 1979. *Word processing fundamentals.* New York: Harper & Row.

Waterhouse's book is one of the better text books on the market.

WATKINS, J. K. 1981. WP performance indicators. *Words* 9 (6, April-May):36-38.

Watkins tells how to develop departmental objectives and gives examples, in the context of a case study, of objectives for customer satisfaction; cost effectiveness; productivity improvement; staff performance, opportunities, and attitude; and innovation.

WEST, T. W. and MULLINS, C. J. 1981. Word processing in a major university: Policies, plans, and management. *Management Information Systems Quarterly* 5 (December):1-18.

This paper summarizes policies, plans, management, and study tools for planners of word processing systems.

WILSON K. 1980. Blind operators achieve despite the odds. *Words* 8 (6, May-June):20-26.

This article explains from case studies how the blind can become competent word processing operators with the aid of technology, open-minded employers, and ambition.

WOLF, C. L. 1981. Low-cost word processing for TRS-80 users. *onComputing* 3 (1):43-46.

This article will interest readers who want word processing for home use, either personal or professional. The system uses a standard selectric typewriter for printing.

WOHL, A. D. 1981a. Office of the future—close but still elusive. *The Office* 93 (1, January):93-94, 190.

Wohl points to gradual changes in modern office planning. She sees more adaptation to traditional office patterns, with equipment becoming cheaper and more functions being performed on it; word processing expanding into data processing and other areas; and greater interest in office technology by data processing people. In her view, the greatest successes in office technology will go to the firms that make their equipment easiest for nontechnical users to learn.

152

_____. 1981b. Survival tips for multi-function office systems planners. *Words* 9 (4, December–January):26-30.

Wohl, well-known consultant on office systems, predicts the proliferation of systems with many work stations. Her article gives tips on buying such systems. She counsels buyers, among other things, to match their idea of "support" with the vendor's idea because the DP firms that are selling WP software for large mainframes do much less "hand-holding" than WP vendors traditionally have provided.

WOLLMAN, J. 1981. Tune in to teleconferences. *Savvy* (September): 16-20.

Wollman weighs the pro's and con's of teleconferencing, explaining details and techniques. She speculates on whether teleconferencing will become a means to reduce travel or, instead, an expensive substitute for telephone calls.

1980. Word and text processing at Indiana University: Direction and Plans. Unpublished report. Bloomington, Indiana: Office of Information and Computer Services, Indiana University.

1981. Word processors are boon to this one-man law firm. *The Office* 93 (2, February):102.

This article, on word processing in a very small firm, will interest owners and managers of small businesses.

ARTICLES ON MICROCOMPUTING SOFTWARE

HART, G. A. 1980. Magic Wand word processor. *Creative Computing* 6 (8, August):38-45.

This article thoroughly reviews one of the best software packages, the programmable Magic Wand, renamed "Peach Text" in 1982.

JONG, S. 1981. Word processing software round-up. *Personal Computing* V (1, January):26-33.

This article reviews software packages for the Apple, Commodore Pet, and TRS-80 as well as several text formatting packages.

1981. Personal computers: Word processing packages. *The Seybold Report on Word Processing* 4 (4, April):1-16.

This thorough review of word processing packages, available from Seybold Publications, Inc. (Box 644, Media, PA, 19063), doesn't cover all the available packages but does give prospective purchasers a solid sense of what microcomputer word processing is like.

PRESS, L. 1980. Word processors: A look at four popular programs. *onComputing* 2(1, Summer):38-52.

This excellent article reviews Magic Wand, WordStar, Electric Pencil, and Auto Scribe software.

Index